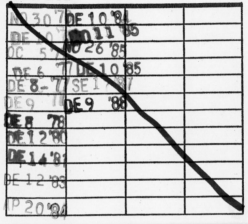

Equal Justice

THE WARREN ERA
OF THE SUPREME COURT

Arthur J. Goldberg

1971 ROSENTHAL LECTURES
Northwestern University School of Law

FARRAR, STRAUS & GIROUX
New York

Copyright © 1971 by Northwestern University Press
Library of Congress catalog card number: 72–167921
ISBN 0-374-51000-8
First Noonday edition, 1972
All rights reserved
Printed in the United States of America

For my children and grandchildren,
who I trust will enjoy the blessings
of liberty under the rule of law,
and who I am sure will always remember
the wise counsel of Thomas Paine:
"Those who expect to reap the blessings
of freedom must . . . undergo the
fatigue of supporting it."

And for my wife.

Preface

Emblazoned on the portals of the great edifice that houses the Supreme Court of the United States are the words "Equal Justice under Law."

Equal justice was an unrealized goal when the "marble palace" was erected in the 1930s; it is still unrealized. It is the thesis of this book that great progress was made toward the realization of equal justice during the years in which Earl Warren served as Chief Justice of the United States.

No one can guarantee that this progress will continue or that backward steps will not be taken. I can only express the conviction that the Supreme Court will continue to do its part in the "sacred stir toward justice" and that "the flame will burn bright while the torch is in [its] keeping."

Among those who share this hope are the gifted law professors and practicing lawyers who served as my law clerks during my tenure on the Supreme Court. They have given generously of their time and skill in assisting in the preparation of the lectures from which this book derives. I wish, in particular, to express appreciation to Stephen Breyer, Alan Dershowitz, David Filvaroff, and Daniel Levitt, whose insights proved invaluable in my analysis of the contribution of the Warren Court.

I am also very much indebted to Kevin M. Clermont and H. Barry Vasios, third-year students at Harvard Law School, and Larry Elliot Shapiro, a third-year student at Georgetown Law Center, who with enthusiasm and ability lent their efforts to documenting my thesis about the Court. I also want to thank my son Robert, and my son-in-law, Dr. David Cramer, for reading the manuscript and for their most helpful suggestions as to both readability and content.

My debt to my secretaries, Norma Garaventa and Jane Merrill, is also very great. They transcribed and typed the manuscript with dispatch and accuracy notwithstanding their busy regular work schedule.

I conclude by saying that I alone am responsible for the views expressed and conclusions drawn and for whatever the shortcomings of the book may be.

ARTHUR J. GOLDBERG

Contents

i x

I

A Court
of Relevant Justice

THERE ARE RESPECTS in which the Warren Court was unlike any which had preceded it.[1] Every Court is, of course, in part a product of its time. John Marshall's Court was of necessity required to give life to the fresh language of a new Constitution. Whether by action or inaction—and it chose action—the Court was largely to determine what emerged from our great experiment in nation-making.

By mid-century the Court was called upon to face the sectional strife which was tearing the nation apart. The Court failed, as Dred Scott [2] bears tragic witness. It spent the rest of the century in resolving, or evading, the challenges posed by the violent end of slavery, the impact of an unprecedented industrial and commercial revolution, and the expansion of the nation across the continent. In the first half of the twentieth century, the rise of organized labor, the transformation of the nation into an urban society with a strong centralized government, and unprecedented economic crisis provided the background of the Court's work.

It is not surprising, therefore, that Marshall's Court focused upon nation-building, that Taney wrestled with sectionalism, that Chase, Waite, and Fuller led Courts which largely serviced the legal needs of economic expansion, and that the Courts presided over by Taft, Hughes, and Stone were required to devote much of their energy to reconciling our conventional wisdom about the role of government in economic affairs with the need to enable society to survive the world-wide economic crisis.

By the 1950s, nation-building, sectional strife, and the economy were lower on the agenda—or transmuted into other issues. There were new questions for the Court—whatever the predilections or views of its members. The disposition of the problems of the past had turned attention to other, long neglected ones. Concern about these new problems was, in part, the result of the failure to effectively resolve the old ones. Neither the Court nor the country had dealt successfully with the aftermath of civil war; the slaves had been made "free," but the shackles and heritage remained. Business and then government had been permitted to grow and become powerful, but their relation to the rights of individual citizens had not been carefully defined or controlled. Literacy and even university education were widespread. New media of communication turned ideas into causes and local developments into world-wide concerns. And the technological revolution not only threatened to further weaken the effectiveness of the individual, but also accustomed us to more rapid change.

It was no longer possible for the Court gingerly to enter upon a problem, then to wait for a generation until its handiwork had been tested in experience. Changes in the nature of the bar, for example, precluded such a leisurely pace. Litigating organizations like the National Association for the Advancement of Colored People, and the American Civil Liberties Union, and—later—various kinds of poverty law groups pressed the Court with cases raising every facet of every important social problem. Such was the milieu in which the Warren Court labored. The present and future Courts will necessarily face issues posed by public interest lawyers pressing environmental, ecological, and consumer issues—and this is all to the good.

To me, the major accomplishments of the Court during the fifteen years in which Earl Warren was Chief Justice were a translation of our society's proclaimed belief in racial equality into some measure of legal reality, the beginning of a profound change in the mechanics of our political democracy and the revolution in criminal justice, both state and federal.

The areas of advancement were varied, but generally the Court sought to bring legal rules into consonance with the human reality to which they purport to respond.

In the reapportionment cases, the Court realized that the failures of the other branches of government had left the judiciary with the task of fulfilling the Constitution's promise of equality in our representative system of government. In *Baker v. Carr*,[3] *Reynolds v. Sims*,[4] and subsequent cases, the Court succeeded in moving the nation toward the ideal in which every man's voice is equally authoritative in determining how he is to be governed.

In the civil rights cases,[5] the Warren Court gave a new lift to the Civil War Constitutional Amendments, provided the moral leadership, and clarified values and ideals for a country that had shown itself to be sorely in need of such guidance. The problems of racial discrimination are far from solved, but, within the limits of its institutional capacity, the Court has contributed to the progress toward a solution.

In the realm of criminal justice the Court asserted its faith in the continuing viability of the Bill of Rights. Although our criminal system is far from perfect, today we are at least started along the path toward equal justice for all, be they poor or rich, be they tried by state or federal government.

In the following pages, I shall touch briefly upon all of these themes; the advances made by the Warren Court provide rich source material. I shall focus first on the last area mentioned, namely, criminal justice, perhaps because the decisions in this area are the most controversial. I will attempt to explain the advances made, to justify the overrulings necessary to these advances, and to demonstrate why the Warren Court's decisions should stand. For a variety of reasons, the Warren Court's criminal justice decisions are most vulnerable to attack. In the first place, there is a great—and in many respects justified—concern about the increase in crime. The fact that this increase has coincided with an expansion of constitutional safeguards for criminal defendants has led some critics to assume—erroneously, in my view—a relationship between the two. Moreover, "take the handcuffs off the police" is a profitable political slogan, and the courts are a convenient scapegoat on which to place the blame for our inability to solve frustrating and difficult social problems. Further, there are already efforts afoot to ask the Court to reverse or limit various criminal justice decisions. Finally, there are a number of scholars —in the academies and on the bench—who are urging this course on the Court.

By comparison, most of the other fronts on which the

Warren Court moved forward are relatively secure. The reapportionment decisions, despite early efforts to undo the Court's work by constitutional amendment, are now so secure that they have been called the "success story of the Warren Court." [6] The moral considerations underlying the civil rights cases are so clear and compelling that some elected officials from states which resisted these decisions most defiantly are now supporting compliance. The remaining civil rights questions—very important, to be sure—involve the speed and detail of further implementation. And the cases involving freedom of speech, press, assembly, and privacy are helped by the fact that many people are beginning to see that the advances are aimed at protecting them. Most people hold at least one view which is controversial and which others would rather not have them express. Moreover, the press—with its enormous resources—has, for understandable reasons, championed the right to express one's views without fear of censorship—witness the virtually unanimous and justified press view concerning their right to publish the Pentagon Papers without prior restraint—and we all like our privacy and want it respected.

But the rights of the criminal defendant do not share the majoritarian popularity of the reapportionment cases, the compelling morality of the civil rights cases, or the emerging popular appeal of the free speech, press, and privacy cases. Accordingly, it is the criminal justice cases which deserve the special attention I propose to devote to them.

The Warren Court's advances in criminal justice fall into a number of fairly distinct groupings, of which I will discuss four. The first grouping consists of those cases in which the Warren Court sought to eliminate the invidious effects of poverty on individuals' constitutional rights when facing the administration of justice. This type of category is perhaps best explicated by example.

Before 1956, Illinois provided appellate review of criminal convictions. But in preparing an adequate record for appeal, the defendant was faced with the practical necessity of procuring a trial transcript. This expensive requirement created an almost insuperable obstacle to the indigent's access to the appellate process. Accordingly, the Court in *Griffin v. Illinois* [7] held that if a state provided an appeal process, all defendants, rich or poor, must have equal access. Therefore, Illinois had to provide a free transcript to the indigent defendant who wished to appeal. The logic of this decision was well summed up in the Court's opinion:

> There can be no equal justice where the kind of trial a man gets depends on the amount of money he has. [8]

The impact of this simple—and, in retrospect, obvious—decision was profound and dramatic. Numerous indigent defendants who—under the prior practice—could not have appealed, succeeded in their appeals and had their convictions reversed.[9]

A second example is the Warren Court's defense of the right to counsel for the poor. The preeminent position that the right to counsel has enjoyed in our jurisprudence since the birth of this nation is easily understood. It is based on the recognition that our trial system is adversary in character and complex and confusing to such a degree that, without the guidance of counsel, all the varied procedural safeguards evaporate into meaninglessness. As Dean A. Kenneth Pye has noted, "The game is quite different when each side has a goalie." [10]

In accordance with this basic characteristic of the adversary process, appointment of counsel for the poor had long been required in federal trials; [11] but prior to 1963 it was not deemed constitutionally required in state trials.[12] Then along came Clarence Earl Gideon, whose request for counsel had been denied in his felony state court trial in Florida. The outcome of this case was the absorption of the Sixth Amendment, making it obligatory on the states to provide the poor defendant the assistance of counsel, at least in trials for felonies.[13] Though the tools of effective advocacy—such as investigators, psychiatric and other experts—are still denied to the poor in many jurisdictions, counsel can, at least, call such inequalities into question and set in process a continuing challenge to unequal treatment of the poor.

The impact of this decision was also considerable. Many defendants, including Gideon himself, who had been convicted without counsel, were acquitted upon retrial with a lawyer.[14]

A second category of criminal procedure cases were those aimed at safeguarding and effectuating already-recognized rights. This was done in two ways: either by assuring that the recognized rights could be effectively exercised or by providing a remedy for violation of those established rights. These two paths to a common goal are exemplified by *Escobedo v. Illinois*[15] and *Mapp v. Ohio*.[16]

Danny Escobedo, it may be remembered, was suspected of being implicated in his brother-in-law's murder. He was arrested, interrogated, and then released on a state court writ of habeas corpus secured by his retained counsel. Subsequently, after his co-suspect told the police that Escobedo had fired the fatal shots, Escobedo was again arrested and importuned to confess. His request to consult with his lawyer was denied. And his lawyer's request, made in person at the police station, to meet and advise his client was met first with evasiveness and then with refusal. Escobedo was then confronted with his co-suspect, who accused him of the killing. This presented him with a dilemma. Would his silence in the face of such an accusation be taken as an admission by silence? Having been denied access to his lawyer for advice in this delicate situation, although his lawyer was just outside in the corridor, Escobedo told his co-suspect in the presence of the police and prosecutor, "I didn't shoot Manuel, you did it," thus indicating knowledge of and participation in the crime.

I wrote the opinion for the Court applying the Gideon decision to the stage "when the process shifts from investigatory to accusatory—when its focus is on the accused and its purpose is to elicit a confession." [17] Any other result would, I said, "make the trial no more than an appeal from the interrogation. . . . [18] One can imagine a cynical prosecutor saying: 'Let them have the most illustrious counsel, now. They can't escape the noose. There is nothing that counsel can do for them at the trial.' " [19]

As subsequent events have apparently pointed up, Danny Escobedo is not exactly a model citizen. The majority of those who are protected by the criminal justice decisions of the Warren Court may not be nice people. But I need not state how irrelevant that must be in a system of constitutional safeguards. As Winston Churchill, then Home Secretary, said in a speech delivered in the House of Commons on July 20, 1910:

> The mood and temper of the public in regard to the treatment of crime and criminals is one of the most unfailing tests of any country. A calm, dispassionate

recognition of the rights of the accused, and even of the convicted criminal, against the State—a constant heart-searching by all charged with the duty of punishment—a desire and eagerness to rehabilitate in the world of industry those who have paid their due in the hard coinage of punishment: tireless efforts towards the discovery of curative and regenerative processes: unfailing faith that there is a treasure, if you can only find it, in the heart of every man. These are the symbols, which, in the treatment of crime and criminal, mark and measure the stored up strength of a nation, and are sign and proof of the living virtue within it.

As should be obvious, my categories of cases are not mutually exclusive. *Gideon v. Wainwright* [20] is a prime example of the Court's attempt to eradicate the effect of poverty on justice; yet, being a right to counsel case, it was also aimed at maintaining a situation in which the other rights guaranteed by the Bill of Rights—such as confrontation and exclusion of illegally obtained evidence—could be exercised. Similarly, *Miranda v. Arizona* [21] is a case which bridges these first two categories. In it, the Court applied the *Escobedo* holding to the indigent situation. Ernesto Miranda did not have his lawyer waiting in the station house. But recognizing that the need for counsel, in order to protect the accused's constitutional rights, is very strong even at the early stages of prosecution, the Court held that the states were constitutionally required to make known at the interrogation stage the availability of the assistance of counsel for the indigent suspect.[22]

Turning now to the other subtype of my second category, we come to the cases providing a remedy for recognized rights. As early as 1949, in *Wolf v. Colorado*, the Court had decided that the Fourth Amendment guarantees were "implicit in 'the concept of ordered liberty' and as such enforceable against the States through the Due Process Clause."[23] However, *Wolf* left the remedy for violations of the Fourth Amendment up to the states. Finally, in 1961, the Court recognized that the states had failed to enforce the right and realized that, in fact, the exclusion from evidence of the fruits of an illegal search and seizure was the *only* effective and suitable remedy to vindicate Fourth Amendment rights. Thus, in *Mapp v. Ohio* the federal exclusionary rule was held

an essential ingredient of the right newly recognized by the Wolf case. . . .[24] [W]e can no longer permit that right to remain an empty promise.[25]

The third grouping of cases rearticulated and rationalized the bounds of recognized rights. Here the Court did not clearly move either forward or backward: it merely attempted to spell out and define. Its efforts in this direction are, of course, still in process, since no Court can or should fix for all time the developing application of the safeguards of the Bill of Rights. The law is not settled, for example, as to what constitutes an illegal search and seizure under all circumstances in a technological age. It is in the nature of the Fourth Amendment, whose operative terms included "reasonable," to be less absolute than other amendments whose terms are more precise. Future Courts must contribute to the ongoing definitional process.

For another example from the Fourth Amendment, we may turn to the 1967 decision in *Katz v. United States*.[26] Prior to that case, an illegal search and seizure required a physical "intrusion or trespass" [27] into a "constitutionally protected area." [28] In *Katz* the petitioner had been convicted on the basis of evidence obtained by attaching an electronic listening and recording device to the *outside* of a *telephone booth*. Prior doctrine would evidently condone this invasion of privacy. But "[t]ime works changes, brings into existence new conditions and purposes." [29] The change worked here was what Justice Brandeis termed "the progress of science in furnishing the Government with [new] means of espionage." [30] Accordingly, in *Katz*, the Court adopted a purposive rearticulation of the compass of the Fourth Amendment which is suited to the safeguards of our citizens in the modern day. Rejecting the "constitutionally protected area" approach, the Court concluded that the Fourth Amendment

> protects people, not places. What a person knowingly exposes to the public, even in his home or office, is not a subject of Fourth Amendment protection. . . . But what he seeks to preserve as private, even in an area accessible to the public, may be constitutionally protected. . . .[31] [Moreover], it becomes clear that the reach of that Amendment cannot turn upon the presence or absence of a physical intrusion into any given enclosure.[32]

Nor could the reach of the Amendment turn, as it had, on whether an arrest occurred in a house or on the street.

The old test for a search incident to arrest, set out in *United States v. Rabinowitz*,[33] was vague; it was "not whether it is reasonable to procure a search warrant but whether the search was reasonable." This test had been so broadly interpreted as to push the Fourth Amendment protection to the "evaporation point." Accordingly, on Chief Justice Warren's last day on the bench, the Court handed down its decision in *Chimel v. California*[34]—a decision which provided a relatively clear and purposive standard by which to test the reasonableness of searches incident to arrest. The Court invalidated a warrantless search incident to petitioner's arrest in his home; the search had covered the attic, the garage, and a small workshop, as well as the entire three-bedroom house. The Court could find no constitutional justification for allowing anything but

> a search of the arrestee's person and the area "within his immediate control"—construing that phrase to mean the area from within which he might gain possession of a weapon or destructible evidence.[35]

A third example of rearticulation was the elimination of the "mere evidence" rule by *Warden v. Hayden*.[36] Previously, the Court had ruled [37] that only smuggled goods, the fruits and instruments of crime, and contraband articles could be seized—mere evidence could not. The rejection of this rule in the *Warden* case was based on a recognition that

> the principal object of the Fourth Amendment is the protection of privacy rather than property, and [we] have increasingly discarded fictional and procedural barriers rested on property concepts.[38]

This decision tends to rebut the argument that the Warren Court *always* redefined constitutional rights in order to expand them in favor of the accused. The Court showed here the same realism that resulted in *Katz;* the old "mere evidence" rule protected no valid interests, and in fact gave no practical protection at all—the Supreme Court had not declared evidence inadmissible under the rule since 1921,[39] and lower courts were likewise able to avoid that result by simply perverting the meaning of "instrument" of crime. I do not mean to commit myself to a defense of the overruling necessary to the decision in *Warden v. Hayden*, but only to point out that its effect was not a significant contraction of existing Fourth Amendment rights.

The fourth and last category of cases comprise those aimed at providing roughly equivalent constitutional safeguards in state and federal courts. Here the Warren Court was merely continuing a tradition dating back to the 1908 decision in *Twining v. New Jersey*;[40] I refer "to the process by which fundamental guarantees of the Bill of Rights are absorbed by the Fourteenth Amendment and thereby applied to the States." [41] By this process

> the Court has held that the Fourteenth Amendment guarantees against infringement by the States the liberties of the First Amendment, the Fourth Amendment, the Just Compensation Clause of the Fifth Amendment, the Fifth Amendment's privilege against self-incrimination, the Eighth Amendment's prohibition of cruel and unusual punishments, . . . the Sixth Amendment's guarantee of the assistance of counsel

for an accused in a criminal prosecution [42] . . . and the Sixth Amendment's right of confrontation.[43]

The Court accepted

> that the genius of federalism does not require that states be permitted to experiment with the fundamental rights of defendants. . . . The mere status of being in America should confer protection broad enough to protect any man from the vagaries of a state which by inertia or design fails to keep pace with a national consensus concerning the fundamental rights of the individual in our society.[44]

This categorization suggests that advancement of the criminal defendant's constitutional rights during the Warren years was not as great a departure from the past as the Court's critics would have us believe. Ensuring equal treatment for the rich and poor and for the federal and state defendant, rearticulating and redefining previously recognized rights without moving markedly forward or backward with respect to the expanse of those rights—none of these aims seems unreasonable. The Warren Court concentrated on strengthening the defenses of the individual's rights—entrenching along boundaries already set out long ago. In fact, what the Court was doing can be justified on strict constitutional and stare decisis grounds, as I will show later.

For the most part, the Warren Court's criminal law decisions did not undercut legitimate reliances. No policeman could legitimately rely on the absence of an exclusionary rule. He knew—or should have known—that the primary conduct whose fruits are now excluded was already forbidden by prior decisions. Nor could he legitimately rely on the defendant's lack of information or resources necessary to effectuate already established rights and safeguards.[45]

But to say that legitimate reliances were not undercut is not to downgrade the fundamental nature of the Warren Court's criminal law decisions. They were fundamental precisely because they were not a mere extension of preexisting rights. They introduced an entirely new principle—a new promise—that where there is a right, that right will not remain unenforceable because of the defendant's poverty, ignorance, or lack of remedy. These decisions lie close to the essence of our great constitutional liberties. The changes that were made were intended to adapt these rights to changed circumstances, to ensure that they did not lose their meaning in a new society, to enable their continued, effective exercise in the spirit of equality, and to allow them to meet new evils and impediments that the framers did not know. In sum, the changes were designed to give practical effect to the protections afforded by the Bill of Rights and to deal with the realities of the varying situations

confronting the Court in the area of criminal justice.

Turning to the area of racial discrimination, many believe *Brown v. Board of Education* to be the most significant decision of the Warren Court. The literature on *Brown* is so extensive that it would be fruitless to add my views to what has been said on its merits, although I agree wholeheartedly with the decision and its rationale.[46] It will perhaps suffice to record my conviction that *Brown* had a momentous impact as a legal signpost pointing toward the elimination of all kinds of legal barriers based on race and as a social landmark from which broader changes in black-white relations can be dated. But I choose to discuss *Brown* for another reason. I use it as exemplary of a more subtle trend of constitutional adjudication, as an indication of an attitude by the Warren Court to focus on issues in a different way.

In deciding *Brown* the Court cut through the fiction surrounding the old "separate but equal" doctrine to the realities which had always been patently obvious to all who were willing to see: that "separate" could never be "equal," because its very genesis and its only purpose for being was to be invidiously discriminatory, to keep the black man in an inferior status. But self-evident as this had always been, it was not until 1954—less than twenty years ago and almost one hundred years after the adoption of the Fourteenth Amendment—that the

Court was willing to accord a full constitutional recognition and significance to an unmistakable reality.

It is this theme I would like to explore a bit further—the Court's move to bring legal rules into consonance with the human reality to which they purport to respond. *Brown* was not the first case in which the Court rejected legal fiction in favor of perceivable fact. I have already referred to criminal justice decisions of like import, but, if belated, *Brown* was more dramatic than the others. And in its wake came the series of cases, the progeny of *Brown*, in which the justices and the lower federal courts have repeatedly been called upon to look through formalistic devices to substance and to strike down or remedy evasive doctrines designed to frustrate both the express mandate of *Brown* and its subsequently articulated constitutional radiation.[47] Never, it seems, has the judiciary been so confronted with such a series of schemes molded to fit mechanical distinctions and thereby to avoid compliance with law: from sham freedom of choice plans to evasive transfers of local public facilities to ostensibly private hands. Many federal courts, and particularly the Supreme Court, to their great credit have by and large shunted the formalisms and cut through to expose faulty and unconstitutional systems.[48]

In no other area, perhaps, has the Court been so ready to measure the actual impact of official conduct as it has with regard to racial discrimination. The justices of the Warren Court were even willing to deal with the racial indignity inherent in the courtroom practice of addressing black witnesses by their first names only, while according whites the courtesy of a "Mister," "Mrs.," or "Miss." [49] This may seem of little moment to some, but it is exceedingly important in recognition of human dignity.

In no other group of cases has the Court been so prepared to dislodge traditional formalisms as when it applied the Thirteenth, Fourteenth, and Fifteenth Amendment prohibitions against racial barriers. This willingness to look at the real impact of governmental action, to search for truth amid the fictions of legal doctrine, has brought a new freshness to constitutional adjudication, a recognition that the basic law must be willing to grapple with everyday reality. And so the Warren Court became a place of particular promise and hope for black and brown people, who were thereby encouraged to believe that racial justice is actually attainable, that the law could understand their own reality in a way which would allow it to frame meaningful relief from the everyday denials of constitutional principle and right.

There were similar emanations from other areas of the law as well—nonracial cases in which the Warren Court favored the actual over the assumed.

In *Reynolds v. Sims*, the great reapportionment decision, Chief Justice Warren, speaking for the Court, said in the most realistic of terms:

> Legislators represent people, not trees or acres. Legislators are elected by voters, not farms or cities or economic interests. As long as ours is a representative form of government, and our legislatures are those instruments of government elected directly by and directly representative of the people, the right to elect legislators in a free and unimpaired fashion is a bedrock of our political system.[50]

In *In re Gault*[51] and its successors, which required that juveniles be afforded counsel and other due process protections, the Court rejected long-standing assumptions about the paternally protected nature of juvenile proceedings; again, the controlling factor was reality—what actually happens to children in our courts.

Even in such a traditionally conservative area as jurisdiction and procedure, the Court recognized the need to face the practicalities of the situation. In *Dombrowski v. Pfister*[52] it expanded the possibilities for federal intervention to restrain state criminal proceedings which threatened constitutional rights. The allowance of immediate injunctive relief in the federal courts was deemed appropriate because of the pragmatic inadequacy of leaving at least First Amendment rights to vindication by the slow process of appeal after conviction through the state court system to the Supreme Court itself.

Elsewhere there was a continuing shift in focus away from a doctrinal inquiry into whether the parties had rights in the old unrealistic legal sense; in its place came an attempt to take hold and measure the real impact of the action being challenged. Thus, in decisions dealing with public assistance programs, there was again perception of the practical importance of government aid programs to welfare recipients—an awareness of the fact that they often meant actual economic or physical survival.[53]

In summary, from these and other cases, it appeared that the Warren Court was manifesting a growing and possibly more general impatience with legalisms, with dry and sterile dogma, and with virtually unfounded assumptions which served to insulate the law and the Constitution it serves from the hard world it is intended to affect. If still not articulated, there was discernible a general groping for what might be called a "new realism" in the Court's approach, a retreat from abstraction and an increased willingness to attach broader significance to the realized human impact in the events that gave rise to legal disputes and court cases. That movement was both healthy and necessary; it responded to an increasingly apparent fact of modern life—the gap, too often a chasm, between the sometimes pietistic pronouncements of our system and its performance in fact.

To me, at least, one of the most crucial challenges facing the Supreme Court today—indeed, confronting our entire system of courts and justice—is the need to make our declared principles, our constitutional protections, into a workable and working reality for those to whom they must often seem to be the sheerest of illusion and promissory deception. Lawyers, teachers, judges, and others have spent decades molding and remolding legal doctrine, shaping it into ever more refined declarations intended to protect human liberty, expand personal freedoms, and enhance individual dignity. But it is of the utmost importance that the words match the practices.

In this time of social change, it seems to me that what the Court must do especially is maintain the perspective of reality perceived by the Warren Court; it must possess and convey an empathy for and understanding of the facts of life for those who come before it as parties and for those whom its mandates would purport to affect. And it is here that a stifling of the new realism would set back the great goal of equal justice under law.

The gap between promise and performance will itself produce many of the most testing constitutional issues for the Court. The new realism offers hope and promise of help in dealing with them convincingly. It will not and cannot be enough for the law to insist on its own fictions and assumptions, or to purport to supply remedies in the form of dramatically declared principle which practice rejects.

X The Supreme Court has recently spoken of courts in general as "palladiums of liberty" and as "citadels of justice." [54] I profoundly believe that the Supreme Court is such a court, and that other lower courts are as well. But we cannot act on the assumption that all courts are or that many are perceived as such. Certainly there are good criminal courts of original and appellate jurisdiction and there are dedicated and well-trained judges who resist the pressures of crowded calendars and work heroically to dispense justice. However, to some elements of our population the judicial system is viewed as anything but a "citadel of justice."

I am not referring to the view taken by those who style themselves revolutionary and who are blind to our constitutional commitment to the rule of law. I am describing the perceptions of some of the residents of our racial ghettos and barrios, of our urban and rural poor, of the economic and socially deprived. These are people to whom the law may seem to be both a mystery and an oppression. They are people whose vaunted "day in court" may well consist of a few minutes—or even a few seconds—before an impatient judge in a dingy courtroom. They are people for whom a plea or verdict of guilty is an inevitable conclusion, for whom the concept of due process may appear to mean no more than completing the paper work necessary to carry out judgment and sentence. And what comes at the end? Having spent six months or a year without bail in a city jail even before the trial, they may be committed to an antiquated prison to spend years in confined and destructive idleness, subject perhaps to ill-trained guards and brutalizing fellow inmates, and governed by a set of arbitrary and subjective rules which can produce additional punishments subject to no fair review. And some of our civil courts are little better.

How can we possibly expect those whose lives are directly or indirectly touched by such a system of justice to share our own deeply held views as to the integrity of our institutional legal process? And, to the extent that our own exhortations ring with commitment to the process and fail to take full measure of the failures of that system, how can we expect our words to be viewed as responsive or less than hypocritical?

The recognition of the disparity between rhetoric and reality is not new; it was always perceivable to those who cared to look. For years, law students encountered a kind of cultural shock when they went from the classroom to the courtroom and discovered that in their day-to-day expressions the courts directly dealing with people did not dispense justice in the way that students learned they should.

Nine justices in Washington, of course, cannot build
new courtrooms or prisons, relieve congested court
calendars, provide rehabilitative services for prisons,
appoint needed new judges or educate old ones to meaningful understanding of the law and their role in it.[55]
But, if the Court cannot "solve" these problems, it is
also true that it cannot avoid them. The problems will
face the Court in the form of constitutional claims concerning rights to speedy trial, to bail, or to treatment
instead of simply a useless confinement after conviction.
They will appear as claims to protection from arbitrary
and unwarranted punishment by prison authorities, and
of entitlement to procedural regularity and decision in
accord with preestablished standards for granting or
denying parole.

It would be disingenuous of me not to concede that
I do have views as to the merits of a number of these
questions; but that is beside the point. Whichever way
the claims might be decided, they cannot be dealt with
adequately unless considered in light of the full and
accurate context from which they arise. Unsupported
assumptions about the good intentions or professional
outlook of judges or prison authorities simply will not
be responsive to the claims being made; abstraction from
fact will not serve, except to increase the distance between declared law and reality and to heighten the
mistrust of the legal system already felt by too many

who are subject to its domain. If the Court is to retain its position at the apex of a relevant system of courts and law, it must confront squarely the practical facts which give rise to the cases it is asked to decide. It cannot ignore the real workings and impact of those institutions for whose substantive and procedural rules and results it bears significant responsibility.

Many such questions will come to the Court in one form or another. For it is true, as Professor Freund has pointed out, that we transform many of our most important and controversial social issues into legal ones. The future of our cities and their teeming populations is one of our most pressing domestic problems and is intertwined with racial and economic aspects. Inevitably, the Supreme Court will become involved.

The United States Court of Appeals for the Fifth Circuit has recently dealt in dramatic fashion with the misallocation of community municipal services.[56] It found a constitutional violation in Shaw, Mississippi, where city authorities had provided white neighborhoods with lights and paved streets and left the black area to live with darkness and mud. The implications of this ruling are manifold and broad, and the Supreme Court will be asked, I am sure, to treat with them sooner or later.

The Court has thus far refused to discuss the constitutionality of unequal public expenditures for education of children in poorer and richer areas.[57] But the issue will rise again, I am sure, with respect not only to the number of dollars support per pupil, but with regard to disparities in the quality of education provided even when there is no great gap in spending. And there will be need to further and more definitively face the issue of so-called de facto segregation in schools and in housing. The Court will be called upon to explain also its thoughts about the relation between those who administer government programs and dispense its funds and those who receive them. Whether the challenges in the welfare area will continue, I do not know. But one thing seems certain. The Court cannot escape the problems raised by *Wyman v. James*[58] and like cases.

Let me suggest finally that the judicial responses which purport to resolve legal and constitutional claims—either affirmatively or negatively—without considering the reality from which the claims spring and in which the claimants live cannot fit the requirements of a relevant justice.

It was one of the great virtues of the Warren Court that it brought to constitutional adjudication a common-sense willingness to deal with the hard and often unpleasant facts of contemporary life.

II

Judicial Activism
and Strict Constructionism

WITH RESPECT TO safeguarding civil liberties, the Warren Court's progress can be measured by comparing the atmosphere that prevailed at the time of Earl Warren's retirement with that prevalent when he came to the bench. Although we still have further to go, no one can dispute that, in the Warren era, we certainly came far from the McCarthyism of the early nineteen fifties to a society in which one can think, speak, write, and associate as one pleases. Since some of the Warren Court's civil liberties decisions are being challenged, I now propose to discuss the question of the basic attitude with which the Court should approach claims that fundamental personal liberties are infringed. How should the Court deal with new factual and legal circumstances involving conflict between human freedom and governmental power? How should the Court face new challenges to personal liberty? To what extent should it embody in its decisions new and developing notions of what constitutes unequal and unfair treatment of minorities? Should it exercise its mandate to protect basic constitutional rights forcefully or should it hesitate to strike down even the most unwise restraints that bind men's freedom?

This question of attitude is one of the most important questions to ask about any court, past, present, or future. In dealing with this question, I shall discuss "strict construction" and "judicial restraint." I shall argue that neither the appeal for "strict construction" nor the philosophical underpinnings of "judicial restraint" warrants any fundamental change in the approach taken by the Warren Court in civil liberties matters. The Court's proper role is to apply the Constitution as it believes that document was meant to apply. It ought not, for either philosophical or political reasons, hesitate to enforce those guarantees of fundamental personal liberty that the Constitution contains. And I believe that history shows that the Supreme Court that is courageous in this regard—the Court that has refused to temper its protection of basic personal liberties for fear of the reactions of others—is the Court that has served its appropriate and necessary role in the framework of our constitutionally ordained system of government.

I hesitate to speak of the debate over judicial attitude in terms of "strict" versus "broad" construction. By "strict constructionist" the critics seem to mean Supreme Court justices who will interpret the phrases of the Constitution literally, applying them in accordance with the intent of the men who framed them. Nonetheless, I believe that it is not profitable to speak of justices as strict constructionists. And I shall explain why.

For one thing, nearly every justice considers himself a strict constructionist in the sense that he tries to apply the Constitution in accordance with the intent of the framers. But that intent is not always easy to ascertain; historical materials rarely point unambiguously to a single, particular disposition for an individual case. In *United States v. Barnett*,[1] for example, after studying the history of the Seventh Amendment, I concluded that the Constitution requires a jury trial in all nontrivial cases of criminal contempt. Justice Clark, speaking for a majority of the Court, reached a somewhat different conclusion. And, in the "sit-in" cases for equal accommodation,[2] I read the history of the Fourteenth Amendment with great care and came to believe that its framers intended that it serve to guarantee equal public accommodation for all without the necessity for congressional legislation, although it did not exclude congressional implementation. Justice Black also read the history of that amendment and came to the conclusion that the Fourteenth Amendment by itself did not guarantee "equal protection," although he too did not preclude congressional action in this area. In light of the broad, general language of the Fourteenth Amendment, it is not surprising that two justices could read it and reach different conclusions. It would be surprising, however, if either Justice Black or I believed that we were justified in disregarding the intent of the framers. We did not.

Historical materials are sometimes ambiguous on the question of whether the framers intended a particular constitutional provision to be interpreted "statically" or "dynamically." That is to say, the framers may have believed that a given factual situation lay outside the scope of protection in 1789 or 1868, and yet they may have been fully aware of the likelihood that, as circumstances change, the same factual situation will later fall within the scope of protection. They may have fully intended for the Constitution to apply in this fashion. For example, the framers of the "cruel and unusual punishment" clause may have believed that whipping in the eighteenth century was neither cruel nor unusual. Yet they may have intended that the clause outlaw whipping as men came to accept more civilized concepts of proper punishment, and, indeed, that it outlaw the death penalty today as unconstitutional by contemporary standards. To take another example, some constitutional experts believe that the framers of the Fourteenth Amendment did not expect it to apply to miscegenation statutes or to discrimination against women. Yet, we now recognize that laws forbidding blacks to marry whites or prohibiting women from serving on juries constitute arbitrary discriminations. Did the framers intend the Fourteenth Amendment to be interpreted "dynamically" so that it encompasses our greater awareness of the meaning of equality? Or did they intend a static interpretation that would freeze certain nineteenth-century notions of some of what is actually arbitrary into the Constitution? I believe they intended the former approach—one that would give full scope to the amendments' application.

Another reason for doubting that critics in fact want the Court to construe the Constitution "strictly" is that any serious effort to label some justices "strict constructionists" reveals that those whom the label most easily fits are unlikely to suit the taste of many of the Warren Court's critics. Among the "strict constructionists" we will find the Court's most stalwart champions of individual liberties. The justices of the Warren Court examined state and federal statutes with the greatest care to determine whether they infringed on constitutionally protected fundamental personal rights.[3] Again, the most current case in point is that of the Pentagon Papers, involving the *New York Times* and the *Washington Post*. Without entering into a discussion of the merits, can it be gainsaid that the strict constructionists are the justices of the majority? Indeed, the dissenters complain that they are applying the Constitution too literally.

Many members of the Supreme Court in the 1920s and 1930s might also justly be called "strict constructionists." They bear this label not because they deferred to legislative judgments, hesitating to strike down statutes enacted by Congress or by the states, but precisely because they declared one after another of these statutes unconstitutional. Justice Sutherland was the perfect model of a strict constructionist as he argued, in dissent, that the Court should hold unconstitutional a Minnesota statute, enacted during the depression, that imposed a two-year moratorium on farm mortgage payments. He stated:

A provision of the Constitution, it is hardly necessary to say, does not admit of two distinctly opposite interpretations. It does not mean one thing at one time and an entirely different thing at another time. If the contract impairment clause, when framed and adopted, meant that the term of a contract for the payment of money could not be altered . . . by a state statute enacted for the relief of hardpressed debtors . . . postponing payment . . . because of an economic . . . emergency, it is but to state the obvious to say that it means the same now.[4]

Thus Justice Sutherland's Court might be called a "strict constructionist" Court. But it is not this sort of Court that many present-day critics of the Warren Court would like to see. Justice Sutherland's Court did not hesitate to use its power of judicial review. Rather, it tried to curb the power of the legislatures to enact economic and social legislation. I believe that it was wrong in trying to do so, and I suspect that most of the critics of the Warren Court would agree.

In any event, strict constructionists, conservative or liberal, have tended to be judicial activists. They have exercised their power of judicial review to the full. This is not the sort of Court that present-day critics seek. What they really have in mind is a Court considerably more restrained than the Warren Court in striking down statutes that interfere with personal liberty. They wish to substitute "restraint" for "activism."

"Judicial restraint"—the basic attitude that makes a court most reluctant to overturn legislative judgments—is in some respects a sound philosophy. Review of the constitutionality of acts of other branches of the government is "the gravest and most delicate duty that [the] Court is called on to perform." [5] And, as I indicated for the Court in *Kennedy v. Mendoza-Martinez*, such a review must be conducted with all respect for the powers of other branches. [6] Yet, I still believe that a proper view of judicial restraint applies with far greater force to laws that regulate economic and social matters than to laws that inhibit the exercise of basic personal liberty. In the latter area, where the Court's critics seem most anxious for the Court to exercise "restraint," the Court should be most reluctant to do so.

Modern-day notions of judicial restraint can trace their origins to the dissents of Justice Holmes. Holmes argued vigorously that the Court ought not to substitute its judgment for that of a legislature where economic regulation was at issue. In *Lochner v. New York*, for example, the Court held that a law limiting the work week in a bakery to sixty hours unconstitutionally infringed on "freedom of contract." [7] Justice Holmes, dissenting, stated:

> A constitution is not intended to embody a particular economic theory, whether of paternalism and the organic relation of the citizen to the State or of laissez faire. It is made for people of fundamentally differing views, and the accident of our finding certain opinions shocking ought not to conclude our judgment upon the question whether statutes embodying them conflict with the Constitution of the United States.

Holmes added:

> I think the word liberty in the Fourteenth Amendment is perverted when it is held to prevent the natural out-

come of a dominant opinion, unless it can be said that a rational and fair man necessarily would admit that the statute proposed would infringe fundamental principles as they have been understood by the traditions of our people and our law.[8]

The basic criticism of the Court in the early part of this century is that it did not accept Justice Holmes's philosophy of judicial restraint. A basic criticism of the Warren Court has been that, although it accepted this philosophy when economic regulation was at issue, it did not accept it when it reviewed governmental action that threatens important personal liberties or those that classify on racial grounds. The Warren Court has been accused of proceeding under a two-faced philosophy. This accusation has also led to charges that the Court's justices have simply followed their personal predilections rather than consistently applied principles of law.

In a lecture to the Indian Law Institute at New Delhi in September, 1964, I responded to this criticism as follows:

It has been said that the Court since the late 1930's has unduly expanded the Fourteenth Amendment's protection of personal rights and unduly contracted the effect of the Amendment in cases involving economic regulation. The Court is charged with having created a "double standard." I do not believe that this charge can be sustained if we refer to the intent of the

4 3

Amendment's framers. There is every evidence that the Fourteenth Amendment was intended to protect the slaves newly freed by the Civil War and to protect personal rights in general. There is not a scintilla of evidence in the debates and reports that the Amendment was intended to abridge or curtail the police power of the state in any other way. In the *Slaughter-House Cases*, speaking of the Civil War amendments, the Court said:

"We repeat, then, in the light of this recapitulation of events, almost too recent to be called history, but which are familiar to us all; and on the most casual examination of the language of these amendments, no one can fail to be impressed with the one pervading purpose found in them all, lying at the foundation of each, and without which none of them would have been even suggested; we mean the freedom of the slave race, the security and firm establishment of that freedom, and the protection of the newly-made freeman and citizen from the oppressions of those who had formerly exercised unlimited dominion over him." [9]

And in *Barbier v. Connolly*, the Court said:

"But neither the [Fourteenth] Amendment—broad and comprehensive as it is—nor any other amendment, was designed to interfere with the power of the State, sometimes termed its police power, to prescribe regulations to promote the health, peace, morals, education, and good order of the people, and to legislate so as to increase the industries of the State, develop its resources, and add to its wealth and prosperity." [10]

4 4

These statements by Justices who could rightfully say that the history of these amendments "is fresh within the memory of us all" decisively refute the suggestion—implicit in the "double standard" charge—that the Court has now departed from the Constitution. Rather it is my conviction that the Court, in emphasizing the protection of personal freedoms, has returned to the single standard of the framers. Thus I do not find the current tendency of our Court to use both the Bill of Rights and the Fourteenth Amendment primarily to protect personal rights and liberties either surprising or revolutionary.[11]

To further evaluate this criticism, one must explore the philosophical underpinnings of the concept of judicial restraint. I believe that when we do so, we shall find strong support for the Warren Court's approach. That is to say, there are good reasons for a less restrained judicial attitude—there are stronger grounds for close judicial scrutiny—of governmental action that infringes on constitutionally protected fundamental personal rights.

The rationale for judicial restraint rests in part on basic democratic theory. Justices, after all, are not responsible to the electorate; they are appointed to their posts for life; and their personal views of the merits of legislation may differ radically from popular beliefs of the day. Legislators, on the other hand, are directly responsible to the public; they are democratically elected; and they are more likely to be moved by popular sentiment.

The value judgment implicit in the argument—that popular, democratic judgment is to be preferred to that of the judge—makes good sense when economic regulation is at issue. It is difficult to see why, if a majority of the electorate wishes to regulate aspects of the economic system under which it lives, it should not be free to do so. Nor is there any reason to believe that the judiciary is more capable than a legislature in determining the means appropriate to meet various economic and social ills.

Still, insofar as judicial restraint is rooted in democratic theory, its application is limited. A preference for democratic decision-making will not, by itself, justify restraint when the functioning of that decision-making process is faulty or when the legislation at issue would weaken the democratic decision-making process. Let me illustrate what I mean by describing four, often overlapping, sets of circumstances in which strict judicial scrutiny of governmental action is not only mandated by the Constitution but also is perfectly consistent with that respect for democracy inherent in the notion of judicial restraint.

First, the Court has always more strictly examined legislative enactments that adversely affect those who are not represented in the legislature. A court, for example, might exercise Holmesian restraint in examining an Illinois statute requiring all milk sold within the state to be pasteurized; but surely its suspicions would be aroused were that statute to require that all milk sold must be pasteurized *in Illinois*. In the latter case, courts past and present have examined with some care the importance of the local interest that the law serves, weighed it against the burden that it imposes upon interstate commerce, and looked for a less restrictive means to attain the locally desired end. Why such extensive scrutiny? Fundamentally because the Constitution mandates the maintenance of a nationwide free market. And, as the commerce clause envisaged, Wisconsin farmers have no voice in the Illinois legislature. Thus, a democratic legislative process which offers Illinois residents some hope of defending themselves against unfair treatment offers no such opportunity to the Wisconsin farmer. And it is just where the democratic check falters that the Court must stand ready to examine closely the purpose of and need for the governmental action in relation to the extent to which it impinges upon a constitutionally protected right.[12]

That close scrutiny which may have had its origins in the concept of creating one nation from several separate economic communities today protects personal freedom of movement from interference by states, and it protects the newly arrived resident from discrimination in such matters as the provision of welfare payments.[13] Moreover, the Court's necessary concern for the unrepresented under the equal protection clause should explain the heavy burden placed upon legislatures to justify any law that would limit the voting rights of blacks,[14] of servicemen,[15] or of those too poor to pay a poll tax.[16]

Second, we should expect a Court, concerned that the unrepresented cannot secure fair treatment through the legislative process, to be equally sensitive to threats to the integrity of that process itself. It was natural, then, for the Constitution's framers to desire strong protection for freedom of speech, of the press, and of expression, as well as close judicial examination of any restriction of those freedoms. Democratic theory requires that those potentially in the minority on any issue have the opportunity to convince others of their point of view. Thus, if ideas cannot circulate with perfect freedom, the effectiveness of the democratic check upon unwise, unfair governmental action is weakened.

The need to secure free expression extends not only to "political" speech, but to expression of all kinds. As Reinhold Niebuhr pointed out, in a democratic society "not even the moral presuppositions upon which the society rests are withdrawn from constant scrutiny and reexamination. Only through such freedom can the premature arrest of new vitalities in history be prevented." [17] Moreover, to secure this expression, the Constitution requires that particular care be taken to prevent persecution or suppression of the unpopular political group. Courts, in this safeguarding of free interchange of ideas, are preserving the effectiveness of our democratic political system. Active judicial review in this area is, then, perfectly consistent not only with the views of the Constitution's authors but also with that respect for the democratic process that ordinarily supports an attitude of judicial restraint.

Third, certain legislative enactments force the Court to face squarely what might be called the problem of the "permanent minority." Democratic theory suggests that democracy works best when majorities are formed from continually shifting coalitions. That is to say, each and every citizen who finds himself in the minority on some issues should find himself in the majority on others. As long as minorities can float in this way, majorities will hesitate to treat them unfairly. For he who votes to exploit another today may find himself in a minority subject to exploitation tomorrow.

Democracy will not work well, however, to protect from exploitation an easily identifiable group, say a racial group, that has difficulty forming political alliances and, as a result, finds itself in the minority on many, if not most, important legislative issues. An ill-spirited majority might easily treat such a group unjustly with only limited fear of political reprisal. Thus, one might be particularly reluctant to rely upon the democratic political process to protect such a group from unfair legislation.

The framers of the Fourteenth Amendment knew that blacks would constitute just such a minority group. For that reason they wrote guarantees of fair and equal treatment into the Constitution. That desire of the framers, as well as the political problem that underlies it, provides strong support for the Court's treatment of any racial classification as "suspect" and warranting the most intensive scrutiny.[18] Again, there seems no inconsistency between such an approach and an attitude of judicial restraint where the democratic process does not face a "permanent minority" problem. I might add that this problem does not arise only in regard to racial groups. It underlies in part the First Amendment's guarantee of freedom of association and religion. And I note that the courts are just beginning to grapple with the question of the extent to which the poor constitute a "permanent minority" group.

The "permanent minority" problem suggests a fourth, and related, set of circumstances in which consistency with the purposes of the Constitution requires a departure from an attitude of judicial restraint. When legislators consider laws that would restrict the freedom of particularly feared or hated individuals, such as political dissenters or criminal suspects, they may not, and on occasion do not, take adequate account of the long-term harm caused society by setting restrictive authoritarian precedents. But legislators, like the rest of us, swayed by feelings of the moment, tend to react emotionally to news of rising crime rates. Moreover, we cannot rely upon the few unpopular individuals likely to be affected by restrictive laws to organize politically to fight their passage; nor can or should we rely upon potential criminal defendants to do so. As a practical matter they cannot easily influence legislation. Neither the executives nor the legislatures are noted for their sensitivity to the views or interests of criminal defendants or political dissenters. It was fear that a legislature, swayed by momentary emotion and political pressure, would be unable to take long-term societal harm into account that led the Constitution's framers to embed protection for fundamental personal liberties and scrupulously fair criminal procedure in the Bill of Rights. For the Court to substitute "restraint" for close scrutiny when such liberties are at stake would make the legislature or the executive their ultimate guardian, thereby undermining the purposes of embodying them in a Bill of Rights.

It may appear that this last argument proves too much. Does it also justify close judicial scrutiny of economic regulation? After all, the Court in the 1920s and 1930s believed that it was doing no more than applying the Fourteenth Amendment's protection of "property" to prevent ravages at the hands of "populist" legislatures.

I do not believe, however, that my argument ordinarily extends to legislative regulation of property rights. Legislation affecting property normally regulates economic interest groups of significant size, not isolated individuals without political power. It is merely stating a fact of life to say that economic interests have political influence. They are ordinarily capable of organizing, forming coalitions, and finding access to the legislative process. They are, in other words, able to protect their interests in the political forum in ways that are often unavailable to those injured when personal liberties are infringed. And it is just where, as a practical matter, the democratic political forum cannot adequately protect fundamental liberties that I have argued the Court has a constitutional obligation to provide protection.

In sum, I have tried to show that proper respect for the democratic process—the philosophy that underlies "judicial restraint"—is perfectly consistent with "activism" in some areas, particularly when the rights of minorities or fundamental individual liberties or the health of the democratic process itself are at issue.

My analysis of "judicial restraint" would be incomplete without recognition of one other element that discussions of that doctrine contain. It is often argued that the Court should strike down enactments of the legislature only with the utmost reluctance lest the Court over-extend itself politically and invite public opprobrium and legislative retaliation. The Court's decisions are politically, as well as legally, controversial, it is pointed out. But, since the Court is not popularly elected, it lacks the political support needed to withstand sustained legislative attack from the other branches of government. Thus, it should not provoke the legislative or executive branches by declaring their acts unconstitutional.

The fear of exposing the Court's political weakness is not a new one. It is revealed in the correspondence of William Wirt, a famous constitutional advocate of the 1830s and a one-time presidential candidate. Wirt defended the Cherokee Indians against Georgia's attempts to annex territory guaranteed them by treaty. Before Wirt brought his action in the Supreme Court, he wrote to one of the justices pointing out that a decision in favor of the Cherokees would probably be ignored both by the Georgians and by President Andrew Jackson. Should Wirt expose the Court's inability to enforce its decisions by bringing this action? Is there, he asked, "any thing exceptionable against me either as a lawyer or as a citizen of the United States, in the part I am taking in this case?" [19]

There is no record of a reply. Yet two years later Wirt argued the issue in the case of *Worcester v. Georgia*,[20]

which the Court decided in his favor. Four days after
the decision came down, Justice Story in effect answered
Wirt's question in a letter written to a friend:

> Georgia is full of anger and violence. What she will
> do, it is difficult to say. Probably she will resist the
> execution of our judgment, and if she does, I do not
> believe the President will interfere. . . . The rumor
> is, that he has told the Georgians he will do nothing. I,
> for one, feel quite easy on this subject, be the event
> what it may. The Court has done its duty. Let the
> Nation now do theirs.[21]

I subscribe unhesitatingly to the attitude revealed in
Justice Story's letter. Throughout its history the Court
that has resolutely applied the law without regard to
political popularity has survived any resulting political
storm, though occasionally, as in the "Court-packing"
controversy, it has been forced to trim its sails. In fact,
within a year of the *Worcester* decision both Georgia
and the President had managed to avoid any direct confrontation with the Court; the Court's prestige, for a
series of complicated political reasons, had risen to unprecedented heights; and the Cherokees had won a re-
prieve (though they were soon to be betrayed by means
of a new treaty). On the other hand, when the Court
has made decisions or refrained from making decisions

for political reasons, it more often than not has inflicted a shameful wound upon itself.

The best-known example of a politically motivated decision is in the case of Dred Scott. Chief Justice Taney, in other respects a remarkably fine judge, believed that he might avert a civil war by holding that a former slave was not a person but was property without the right to sue in a federal court.[22] This decision did not serve what its author had conceived as a well-motivated political objective. It hastened, rather than averted, the war. President Lincoln and other northerners announced they would refuse to abide by it. Indeed, the major effect of the Dred Scott opinion was to weaken the power and the prestige of the Court that issued it, and deservedly so.

A notable example of judicial timidity was the Court's disposition of the Japanese evacuation cases. At the beginning of World War II the government removed 110,000 persons of Japanese ancestry—70,000 of whom were American citizens—from their homes in California, Oregon, and Washington and imprisoned them in camps in the Rocky Mountain states. When legal challenges to this removal reached the Court in 1944, the Court held evacuation constitutional. And it held this despite a record without evidence showing a compelling need for the removal and a government brief that seemingly rested its case on little more than the flat assertion that the military

threat of a Japanese invasion made the evacuation necessary. In fact, we now know that if the Court had insisted
that the government produce strong evidence justifying
its action, it would have been unable to do so. By the
time the Japanese were removed from the West Coast,
military authorities no longer believed an invasion likely.
There were no known instances of American-born Japanese aiding the enemy. Indeed, J. Edgar Hoover stated at
the time that "The necessity for mass evacuation is based
primarily upon public and political pressure . . . [not]
on factual data." He believed the government had bowed
before what he termed "public hysteria." [23]

Yet the Court's opinion held that the totally unjusti-
fied removal of more than 110,000 persons from their
homes, without even a hearing, was in accordance with
the Constitution of the United States.[24] I can see no bene-
fit for either Court or country, but only harm, that
flowed from this decision—a decision which Justice
Jackson, in dissent, described as "a loaded weapon ready
for the hand of any authority that can bring forward a
plausible claim of urgent need." [25] I would agree with
Justice Murphy, who argued in dissent that the Court un-
necessarily sanctioned in the name of the Constitution
what was in fact an unjustifiable deprivation of fundamental personal freedom.[26]

Perhaps the most unfortunate retreat in the Court's
history was that taken during the Reconstruction years

to accommodate what the Court conceived to be the "political realities." In *Plessy v. Ferguson*[27] and other cases,[28] the Court undermined the intent of the framers of the Civil War amendments and the Civil Rights acts. It was then that the Court erected the totally discredited doctrine of "separate but equal."

How different the subsequent history of the races in this country might have been had the Court in *Plessy v. Ferguson* adopted the position of Justice Harlan, who in dissent argued wisely that no "legislative body or judicial tribunal may have regard to the race of citizens when the civil rights of those citizens are involved." If only the majority of the Court had heeded the warning of Justice Harlan, the Elder, who, dissenting from the "separate but equal" doctrine, predicated the following:

In my opinion, the judgment this day rendered will, in time, prove to be quite as pernicious as the decisions made by this tribunal in the Dred Scott case. . . . The present decision . . . will not only stimulate aggressions, more or less brutal and irritating, upon the admitted rights of colored citizens, but will encourage the belief that it is possible, by means of state enactments, to defeat the beneficent purposes which the people of the United States had in view when they adopted the recent amendments of the Constitution. . . . The destinies of the two races, in this country, are indissolubly linked together, and the interests of both require that the common government of all shall not permit the seeds of race hate to be planted under the sanction of law. What can more certainly arouse race hate, what more certainly create and perpetuate a feeling of distrust between these races, than state enactments, which, in fact proceed on the ground that colored citizens are so inferior and degraded that they cannot be allowed to sit in public coaches occupied by white citizens.[29]

These words of Justice Harlan are well known to us today when the name of the author of the majority opinion in *Plessy* has fled the memory of all but the historian. Yet, tragically, it is the majority's legacy of distrust and racial bitterness which today we must attempt to overcome.

On the other hand, I believe that Courts that have unflinchingly followed Justice Story's advice to do their duty—Courts that have not hesitated to apply the provisions of the Constitution for fear of political opposition—have and will be remembered in history as great Courts. And I do not believe they will suffer politically from having done so.

It is true that the Warren Court has been bitterly attacked for many of its decisions expanding constitutional safeguards of individual liberties. Yet few attacks could match in bitterness those directed at the Court of John Marshall. What contemporary congressional critic could match the indignation of Georgia's congressman, and later governor, George Troup? On the floor of the House Troup attacked Chief Justice Marshall's opinion in the great case of *Fletcher v. Peck*,[30] an opinion that struck down an act of the Georgia legislature as an unconstitutional abridgment of the "contracts" clause. Troup shouted,

> If, Mr. Speaker, the arch-fiend had in . . . his hatred to mankind resolved the destruction of republican government on earth, he would have issued a decree like that of the judges. Why . . . do the judges who passed this decision live and live unpunished? [31]

Yet John Marshall and his Court survived political attacks, including congressional attempts to limit severely the Court's jurisdiction. And I believe that present-day attacks on the Warren Court will also moderate in time. In fact, many of the attacks have already moderated.

In my view it is far too easy to underrate the strength of the Court and the acceptability of its decisions. We were warned for many years that if the Court attempted to remedy the gross injustice of malapportionment, its decisions would prove unenforceable. Yet, in the past few years we have seen legislatures throughout the country reapportioned. And the judicial rulings in the reapportionment cases seem to have won popular acceptance as being just. In somewhat lesser measure, the same is true of the prayer cases.[32] Moreover, when the Court is under serious political attack, it can rally many defenders. President Roosevelt, after all, was unable to enact his "Court-packing" plan despite a Congress heavily in his political debt and a series of enormously unpopular Court decisions. (Though here, I must add, the Court helped save itself by modifying what I and many others believe was an incorrect approach toward judicial questions involving economic decisions.)

The Court will, in my view, continue to have powerful supporters and popular acceptance as long as it steadfastly maintains its determination to decide cases on principle and refuses to temper its application of constitutional guarantees with fears for its own political well-being. Whatever the justification for avoiding decisions on the merits of a case in other times, the tenor of the modern world demands that judges, like other men, frankly confront even the most controversial and troublesome judicial problems.

I would conclude that there is no justification for the Court to avoid deciding a citizen's substantial claim of constitutional right on the basis that it may injure itself if it decides that case and vindicates those rights. In other words, I would reject that strain of "political self-protection" that underlies theories of judicial restraint. I would subscribe to that judge's creed stated by Lord Mansfield long ago:

I will not do that which my conscience tells me is wrong to gain the huzzahs of thousands, or the daily praise of all the papers which come from the press. I will not avoid doing what I think is right, though it should draw on me the whole artillery of libels, all that falsehood and malice can invent, or the credulity of a deluded populace can swallow. . . . Once for all let it be understood, that no endeavors of this kind will influence any man who at present sits here.[33]

My argument that "judicial restraint" has only limited applicability when the treatment of minorities, the fundamental liberties of individuals, or the health of the legislative process are at issue is of more than purely theoretical interest. The Court has decided many cases involving such issues in the past and will be asked to decide many more in the future.

For one thing, those who are poor, and in particular those who are poor and black, will continue to ask the courts for protection against many different sorts of discriminatory treatment. As I have pointed out above, the Fifth Circuit Court recently held that a town violates the "equal protection" clause of the Fourteenth Amendment when it distributes its municipal services so that in poor black neighborhoods streets are unpaved, unlighted, and without drainage, while in more affluent white neighborhoods the contrary is the case.[34] The Supreme Court also will have to face this sort of issue, as well as the equally difficult question of the extent to which a state can spend more money per capita on the education of some children than on others.

We should also expect our present system of dealing with criminals to generate difficult legal questions. Do judges, in their judicial capacity, for example, as well as legislators, have some responsibility for seeing that our prisons do not remain breeding grounds for further crime? I note that a federal judge in Arkansas has recently ruled that conditions in at least one of the prisons of that state are so bad that imprisonment there amounts to unconstitutional "banishment from civilized society to a dark and evil world" in violation of the Eighth Amendment's prohibition of cruel and unusual punishment. He has ordered the state to reform that prison or to close it down.[35] And, according to newspaper accounts, in Florida a judge, after inspecting conditions in certain jails, ordered that no more than 700 prisoners could be confined in those jails at any one time.

We may also expect to see the Court challenged with new rules and practices that threaten individual privacy. The federal government claims greater power now than ever before to use wiretapping and eavesdropping devices. The government has even claimed the power to use such devices against any American who is labeled "subversive," without first obtaining a warrant from a court. Two lower federal courts have denied this claim,[36] and their rulings are now on appeal.

The issues they raise seem to me ready for adjudication. The courts did not invite those cases, but, having been presented with them, they ought to decide them in accordance with their function as the ultimate guardians of constitutionally protected fundamental rights. I have spoken of the Court's obligation as guardian of our constitutionally protected individual liberties. And I have argued that in that role the Court must act forcefully, and review scrupulously, threatened infringements.

In conclusion, I should like to observe that often too much is expected of the Supreme Court in protecting our liberties, as Judge Learned Hand once reminded us.[37] However, it is equally true that there is always the danger that too little will be expected of the Court in our continuing struggle toward the achievement of that just society which is our goal.

III

Constitutional
Stare Decisis

It was Justice Felix Frankfurter who warned that "judges must be kept mindful of their limitations and of their ultimate public responsibility by a vigorous stream of criticism expressed with candor however blunt."[1] This theme has been echoed in a *New York Times* editorial comment:

> Unlimited public discussion is a primary safeguard of our democracy. The decisions of the Supreme Court are written by men on paper, not by gods in letters of fire across the sky. Critics may distort them but the Court will have to trust the good sense of the people, just as the people trust the good sense of the Court.[2]

During my years on the Court, I occasionally had reason to regret such encouragement of criticism and even to smart under its implementation—while, of course, never doubting its wisdom.[3] Today, in fact, perhaps because I am no longer on the bench, I find *myself* encouraged to say a few words on "limitation" and "responsibility" as part of this ongoing "public discussion."

Over the last decade, much has been made of the necessity of maintaining checks on the Court's power in constitutional interpretation.[4] In order to understand this criticism—especially when it is coupled with cries of impending disaster—it must be put in historical perspective. To be sure, the argument made for constraints has recently increased in volume and intensity; however, one must remember that commentators on the Court have feared an excess of judicial activism since the days of Chief Justice Marshall and *Marbury v. Madison*.[5]

I have already analyzed and rejected some of the arguments for judicial restraint. In making the case for judicial activism I did not mean to assert or imply that the judiciary should be totally unrestrained. Our system, if you will pardon the obvious for the moment, is after all one of checks and balances. The judiciary, like the other branches, needs to be appropriately restrained. Indeed, this necessity is intensified by the inherently counter-majoritarian nature of the Supreme Court or, as it has been phrased, its role as "a deviant institution in the American democracy." [6]

By this I do not mean to concede agreement with Judge Learned Hand [7] and those legal historians who assert that the Court usurped the power to pass on the constitutionality of state and federal laws. I have long maintained [8] that Chief Justice Marshall did not write on a clean slate when he asserted in *Marbury v. Madison* the right and duty of the Court to declare void legislation contravening the Constitution. His action was forecast in the debates at the Constitutional Convention and was urged by proponents as one of the solid reasons for our Constitution's adoption. And the very first Congress, composed of men whose memories of the making of the Constitution were fresh, enacted the Judiciary Act of 1789, which, from that date to this, has expressly authorized the Court to review the constitutionality of state legislation. [9] This enactment was followed shortly by a succession of laws providing for ultimate review by the Court of judgments of the lower federal courts. I agree with Professor Charles Black that "it seems very clear that the preponderance of the evidence lies on the side of judicial review." [10]

I believe that the Court exercises judicial review, therefore, as a consequence of intent as well as tradition; that it is not a usurped power but a part of the grand design to ensure the supremacy of the Constitution as law, supreme law to which all branches of the government—executive, legislative, judicial, state, and federal—are subject. To many this is what the Constitution clearly expresses in its supremacy clause and what it clearly imports by its very nature as a written document defining and limiting legislative and executive powers.[11]

So, all I mean to say by labeling the Court "counter-majoritarian" is to acknowledge that, when it invalidates a law or action as unconstitutional, the Court necessarily "thwarts the will of representatives of the actual people of the here and now; it exercises control, not in behalf of the prevailing majority, but against it." [12] But to make even this limited acknowledgment, which does not reflect at all on the desirability of judicial review since our Bill of Rights is explicitly designed to protect minorities against a majoritarian government, is nevertheless sufficient to establish the need for some restraint, some checks on the action of the Court.

Foremost among these constraints is the requirement of principled adjudication.[13] This "unmistakable thread in the fabric of our law" [14] has been thoroughly explored and elaborated by leading academicians.[15] It implies much: general and neutral principles of law transcending the immediate result, reasoned judgment, analytic coherence, and respect for precedent. Through such principled self-discipline, the Supreme Court has over the

years largely justified its "supreme autonomy" by dem-
onstrating that its decision rests on a level of theory
"abstract[ed] from the common political process." [16]

I use advisedly the expression "*largely* justified." I
readily grant, as I have pointed out above, that the Supreme Court in its long history has made errors and
mistakes; indeed, some have been of almost calamitous
consequence to the country. But I reassert my belief in
the great contribution to the quality of our society and
American life made by the concept of judicial review—
a concept in which the Court is the final arbiter, restrained primarily by the requirement for principled
adjudication and fidelity to the Constitution.

This emphasis on principled adjudication may sound
strange coming from a former justice who sat on the very
Court so often attacked for ignoring the dictates of that
doctrine. But I am not conceding anything to the critics
in this regard. I am incapable of doing so, if only because
I have never wavered in my belief that principled adjudication is a duty no judge can shirk, or, more accurately,
an ideal to which every judge must aspire.

In other words, it was never with this premise of the
critics that I disagreed. Without detracting at all from
their accomplishment of articulating the need for principled adjudication, I must observe that the need ap-
proaches as near to the incontestable as any doctrine in
all of constitutional law. Rather, it was with the critics'

application of their premise—in their findings of fault and deviation—that I at times disagreed.

While I was on the Court I was restrained from voicing my disagreement, but now that the prohibition has been lifted, I must emphatically reject the position that the Warren Court was nonprincipled, or that it ruled by "foot-stamping," [17] or that an "element that courses through [its] opinions . . . is the absence of workmanlike product." [18] I honestly believe that never in the past history of the Court have its members been better trained, worked harder, or availed themselves of better research facilities. And never has a Court applied these resources more consistently or diligently in the service of principle. I agree wholeheartedly with Professor Wright, who in defense posed the following question:

> What Court in the past achieved a higher level of professional craftsmanship than the [Warren] Court? The great opinions of Chief Justice Marshall surely fail the test. Marshall discusses issues not properly before him, he flirts with provocative ideas and then puts them to one side, he resorts to esoteric statutory construction to avoid deciding constitutional questions, and he announces important conclusions without any reasoning to support them.[19]

Even a cursory review of the U.S. Reports clearly reveals a trend in judicial writing which lends further support to my position. The early cases run on for hundreds of pages, yet the opinions are incredibly unreasoned and confusing. At the start of this century the vogue shifted to brief opinions, which shared the same defects of the early cases, only in a mercifully more concise format. The last twenty years have seen opinions beginning again to grow in length, but the difference—the break with the past—is that this is the product of an honest attempt to rationalize and explain the grounds of decision, to link the rule of the case to a principle.

Again, I do not mean to maintain that the Warren Court made no mistakes, but only that its members acknowledged and pursued, with considerable success, the ideal of principled adjudication.

My aim here, having established a need for principled adjudication, is to examine more closely one of its key facets, namely, respect for precedent. As Professor Archibald Cox has observed:

> Ability to rationalize a constitutional judgment in terms of principles referable to accepted sources of law is an essential, major element of constitutional adjudication.[20]

I propose to begin with a general, quasi-jurisprudential consideration of the reasons behind our casting of Janus in the role of a justice—looking to the future but never losing sight of the past. From this general study, I will venture into the realm of application of premise and hence again into the sphere of disagreement with the critics. My concern will be the treatment that the Warren Court's legacy deserves at the hands of future Courts. The conclusion I hope to develop was perhaps best stated long ago: *stare decisis et non quieta movere*, let the decision stand and do not disturb things which have been settled.

Even this brief preview suggests a "credibility" problem, the response to which likewise deserves a preview. The problem is akin to one of estoppel: how can the decisions of the Warren Court expect greater respect than they appeared to pay their restrictive predecessors? Or, equivalently, making my defense of stare decisis at all convincing requires justification of the Warren Court's overrulings. My thesis is that such a justification is fully possible. Those overrulings were in accordance with a general and neutral principle that has long been observed, although, as far as I am aware, it has never before been fully articulated. The principle to which I refer, and which I will develop more fully later on, is that stare decisis applies with an uneven force—that when the Supreme Court seeks to overrule in order to cut back the individual's fundamental, constitutional protections against governmental interference, the commands of stare decisis are all but absolute; yet when a court overrules to expand personal liberties, the doctrine interposes a markedly less restrictive caution.

It is with this principle that I will seek to establish my necessarily dual argument that the Warren Court's civil libertarian decisions were reached without affront to the doctrine of stare decisis and that those decisions cannot now be rejected without such affront.

The doctrine of stare decisis [21] has been called "a natural evolution from the very nature of our institutions." [22] Lacking a comprehensive statement of legal rules, the common law system relied instead upon the courts to rationally develop preexisting, general principles.[23] The aim was uniformity of decision over time and throughout the judicial system. Realization of the aim necessitated narrowing of the judges' discretion to modify the preexisting principles, and this came to be accomplished by the strong presumption against overruling prior decisions that we call stare decisis.

The desire for uniformity was not based solely or even primarily on theoretical grounds; it was sought for some very practical reasons, of which I offer you five familiar ones. First, stare decisis fostered public confidence in the judiciary and public acceptance of individual decisions by giving the appearance of impersonal, consistent, and reasoned opinions.[24] Second, while the respect shown old decisions thus buttressed courts against the world, such respect also induced in fact a greater impersonality of decision and thereby buttressed the judges against their own natural tendencies and prejudices.[25] This pushed us a giant step away from a government of men toward a government of laws.[26] Third, a rule against overruling facilitates private ordering, since settled law encourages reliance at the stage of primary private activity and also helps lawyers in the counseling of that activity. Fourth, stare decisis eases the judicial burden by discouraging suits—potential litigants cannot expect to get a different view from a different judge—and also by facilitating decision once suits are brought. As Justice Cardozo put it:

> The labor of judges would be increased almost to the breaking point if every past decision could be re-opened in every case, and one could not lay one's own course of bricks on the secure foundation of . . . [those] laid by others.[27]

Fifth and last, justice in the case at hand is served by eliminating the injustices of unfair surprise and unequal treatment.

From this listing of the bases of stare decisis, we can for the moment draw two important lessons. One is that these policies behind the doctrine will not be achieved if we only nominally observe the dictates of stare decisis, while narrowly defining the rule of a case in order to distinguish the precedent to tatters.[28] The true *principle* of the precedent must be respected, a duty not to be circumvented by legalistic maneuvers.

The other lesson is that all these arguments carry over in considerable measure to constitutional adjudication.[29] To be sure, some very influential voices have been raised against this application of stare decisis, claiming that the Court "must test its conclusions by the organic document, rather than precedent." [30] For example, Justice Brandeis wrote that "in cases involving the Federal Constitution . . . this court . . . bows to the lessons of experience and the force of better reasoning." [31] However, it must be noted that he wrote this in 1932 and went on to admit that his fear was adherence to old "prevailing views as to economic and social policy which have since been abandoned." [32] Similarly, Justice Douglas, in a 1949 law review article, advocated a flexible approach to constitutional stare decisis; but, again, his concern appeared limited to the situation in which "a judiciary with life tenure seeks to write its social and economic creed into the Charter." [33] And of the forty-eight overruling decisions made during the period which Justice Douglas chose to examine, only four arguably involve civil liberties; and, significantly, these four all overruled restrictive cases in order to expand those liberties.[34]

My scope here is not to take issue on the broad question of the applicability of stare decisis to all of constitutional law but to narrow my focus to the area

7 7

of personal liberties.[35] These fundamental safeguards against excessive governmental power have long benefited from a special status in our constitutional law.[36] In this area, at least, I believe all of the aforementioned bases of stare decisis apply with undiminished force,[37] as do these words from an opinion by Justice Edward White and Justice Harlan the Elder:

> The fundamental conception of a judicial body is that of one hedged about by precedents which are binding on the court without regard to the personality of its members. Break down this belief in judicial continuity, and let it be felt that on great constitutional questions this court is to depart from the settled conclusions of its predecessors, and to determine them all according to the mere opinion of those who temporarily fill its bench, and our Constitution will, in my judgment, be bereft of value and become a most dangerous instrument to the rights and liberties of the people.[38]

For those purists who still object to even this qualified and limited mixing of the terms "stare decisis" and "constitutional law," I would suggest simply reading "respect for precedent" in each place that I write "stare decisis." No one argues that *no* such respect is due; the question is how much. I will attempt to establish that, in the Court's consideration of precedent which generously treated civil liberties, the respect shown should be so great as to render my stare decisis terminology far from amiss.

Moreover, I readily admit that, in treating with the application of stare decisis to constitutional decision-making, there must be some play in the doctrine.[39] If the role of the Court is to develop rationally preexisting principles, this will occasionally necessitate the rejection of one principle so that another can grow.[40] When clearly convinced that precedent is wrong and that "more harm will not be done in rejecting than in retaining" the precedent,[41] justices are absolved from the commands of stare decisis. In short, we cannot demand, or even desire, complete consistency; in Justice Holmes's words, our law "will become entirely consistent only when it ceases to grow." [42] What we *can* demand is that the Supreme Court evidence more than mere disagreement when the justices overthrow precedent.

My efforts so far have been to explain and justify our law's general presumption against overruling, and also to suggest that exceptions to the presumption exist. Perhaps the best way to expand on this notion that overruling is sometimes justified or even mandated is to look at several of the decisions to overrule made by the Warren Court itself, which in a variety of situations deemed stare decisis not to be controlling.[43]

An occasional overruling by the Warren Court is justified by the fact that the precedent in question was

wrong—not only in the justices' view but in an objective
sense. Such is the situation where the old decision mis-
takenly rested on a subsequently repealed act or overruled case, or where the judge had failed to note a
pertinent statute. The Court later called upon to re-
examine such precedent is universally accorded the
power to correct "mistakes of fact" of this kind.[44] A
prime example from the Warren years is *Murphy v.
Waterfront Commission.*[45]

That case held that a state could not, in the absence of
an assurance of both state and federal immunity, compel
a witness to give testimony which might incriminate him
under a federal law. To arrive at that result necessitated
en route the overruling of the contrary holding in *United
States v. Murdock.*[46] In writing the *Murphy* opinion for
the Court, I took great pains to explicate the *ratio
decidendi* of the earlier case. I showed that the Court in
Murdock had itself rejected weighty precedent—cases
with opinions by Marshall [47] and Holmes [48]—in favor of
the "settled" English rule as set out in the 1851 case of
King of the Two Sicilies v. Wilcox.[49] My research dis-
closed that in the *Murdock* case the Court was then un-
aware that this English case had been overruled by a
higher court only a few years later.[50] Accordingly, we
in *Murphy v. Waterfront Commission* were entirely
justified in rejecting the *Murdock* deviation and return-

ing to the earlier Marshall-Holmes view of the "two sovereign" problem.

Another case overruled in *Murphy*[51] was *Knapp v. Schweitzer.*[52] That decision had allowed state authorities to compel testimony incriminating under federal law and was based in part on the nonapplicability of the Fifth Amendment to the states. However, that basis was undermined by *Malloy v. Hogan,*[53] which absorbed the Fifth into the Fourteenth Amendment. *Knapp* was left an anomaly in the law, and we in *Murphy* were thus justified in rejecting it. Having made the fundamental change represented by the *Malloy* absorption (which, of course, must be independently justified), the Court was in duty bound to tidy up the loose ends by overruling the cases that rested on the old rule. We would expect that much from a Court charged with rational development of the law.

While of interest, the *Murphy* rationales are obviously of limited applicability. A more common, general justification—which supported other Warren Court overrulings, including *Malloy*, and to which I have already alluded—lay in the result: individuals' rights were expanded. This is not the paradox it sounds; I am not arguing that result-orientation, the antithesis of principled adjudication, justifies departure from stare decisis or warrants otherwise nonprincipled adjudication. Instead, I refer to a basic characteristic of the role of stare decisis in constitutional law: certain factors weaken the doctrine's commands when the Court moves to expand personal liberties in accordance with the mandate of the Constitution, while stare decisis retains its full vigor or even gains forcefulness in forbidding contraction of liberty. I would like now to examine at some length these certain factors."

Perhaps the most pervasive and persuasive of these is the proposition that the constitutional safeguards of our fundamental personal liberties were instilled with an innate capacity for growth to enable them to meet new evils.[54] This was probably best stated in a passage, often cited by the Warren Court,[55] from an opinion written by Justice Joseph McKenna and harking back to Chief Justice Marshall. The case was *Weems v. United States*, in which the Court struck down as cruel and unusual punishment the imposition of *cadena temporal*, a harsh and inhuman penalty, then used in the Philippines Territory.

> Time works changes, brings into existence new conditions and purposes. Therefore a principle to be vital must be capable of wider application than the mischief which gave it birth. This is peculiarly true of constitutions. They are not ephemeral enactments, designed to meet passing occasions. They are, to use the words of Chief Justice Marshall, "designed to approach immor-

tality as nearly as human institutions can approach it."
The future is their care and provision for events of
good and bad tendencies of which no prophecy can
be made. In the application of a constitution, therefore,
our contemplation cannot be only of what has been
but of what may be. Under any other rule a constitution would indeed be as easy of application as it would
be deficient in efficacy and power. Its general principles would have little value *and be converted by
precedent into impotent and lifeless formulas.* Rights
declared in words might be lost in reality.[56]

Examples of this growth of our safeguards are almost
too obvious and too numerous to merit discussion. The
one that comes first to mind is the equal protection
clause.[57] In the *Slaughter-House Cases* Justice Miller had
this to say for the Court:

> We doubt very much whether any action of a State
> not directed by way of discrimination against the
> negroes as a class, or on account of their race, will ever
> be held to come within the purview of this provision.[58]

But Justice Miller's doubts [59] were soon resolved against
him.[60] The clause has become the champion of the individual's right to equal treatment on a broad front,
including representative government [61] and the administration of criminal justice.[62]

A second example is the Eighth Amendment guarantee

actually involved in *Weems*. The cruel and unusual punishments envisaged by the Constitution were the tortures of the Stuart reign in England, such as burning at the stake, crucifixion, and breaking on the wheel.[63] However, under an express test of "evolving standards of decency," [64] this clause has come to be held violated by expatriation [65] and by imposition of a criminal penalty for narcotics addiction.[66] Such expansion is not revolutionary; instead, it is mere obedience to the wise instruction of *United States v. Classic*, where Justice Stone wrote:

> In determining whether a provision of the Constitution applies to a new subject matter, it is of little significance that it is one with which the framers were not familiar. For in setting up an enduring framework of government they undertook to carry out for the indefinite future and in all the vicissitudes of the changing affairs of men, those fundamental purposes which the instrument itself discloses. Hence we read its words, not as we read legislative codes which are subject to continuous revision with the changing course of events, but as the revelation of the great purposes which were intended to be achieved by the Constitution as a continuing instrument of government.[67]

Just recently the Fourth Circuit Court has held the death penalty for rape, where the victim's life was neither taken nor endangered, to be cruel and unusual punishment.[68] While I am not a prophet, I have utter confidence that, in due time (as for me, preferably sooner than later), we will arrive at an across-the-board declaration of the death penalty as excessively severe under the Eighth Amendment.[69]

The point that growth of our constitutional protections has occurred need not be further belabored. And the point that this growth should occur was well explained by Justice McKenna as a prerequisite to the Constitution's continued relevance in reality. As the classic warning of Chief Justice Marshall goes, "We must never forget that it is a *constitution* that we are expounding." [70] While, of course, the original reference was to expanding governmental power, Justice Brandeis convincingly explained that Marshall's words have a wider application. "Clauses guaranteeing to the individual protection against specific abuses of power, must have a similar capacity of adaptation to a changing world." [71]

To summarize, this first reason why stare decisis does not inflexibly impede expansion of individuals' rights is based on the fact that under our constitutional scheme these rights do and should expand. Overruling is therefore permissible, or rather intrinsically necessary, to facilitate this beneficial expansion, which I have shown to be sanctioned by tradition and reason. If an old case's restriction on personal liberties resulted from the cir-

cumstance that a new "mischief"—of the kind that concerned Marshall, McKenna, Brandeis, and Stone—was
not extant or recognized at the time of decision, then
that case must fall to enable the Constitution to meet the
mischief. The balance of harms and benefits of rejecting
precedent thus swings toward overruling to permit expansion of liberty.

But what happens if, after time has worked its changes,
a majority of nine thinks that the old mischiefs have lost
their toxicity, that it would be desirable to overrule and
thereby contract previously established rights? Standing
in their way is the proper application of stare decisis to
constitutional adjudication. When contraction is at issue,
the innate constitutional capacity for growth of civil
liberties that I have just described obviously does not act
to weaken the traditional commands of stare decisis. In
fact, other factors that I will discuss indicate that the
doctrine gains in strength when the Court contemplates
overruling in order to cut back on personal liberties. In-
cidentally, as I return to the listing of the aforementioned
"certain factors," it is to be noted that these additional
arguments also lend further support to my conclusion
that the Warren Court's expansion of human liberties
did not entail an affront to the doctrine of stare decisis.

The second factor arguing for the uneven force of the
doctrine rests on the contribution of stare decisis to the
all-important efforts of the Court, under the mandate

of the Bill of Rights, to guard against the tyranny of the majority. Professor Jesse Choper has described the Court's role here rather nicely:

> These constitutional guarantees—such as the freedoms of speech and religion, the constitutional rights of those accused of crime, the right to be free from certain racial discrimination—are generally rights of "politically impotent minorities." By definition, the processes of democracy bode poorly for the security of such rights. . . . Thus, the task of guarding these constitutionally prescribed liberties sensibly falls upon a body that is not politically responsible, that is not beholden to the grace of excited majoritarianism—the United States Supreme Court.[72]

The fact that our Constitution has bestowed this essential task on the Court reinforces the previous conclusion that the Court is justified in assuming an "activist" attitude with regard to civil liberties, even when that entails overruling restrictive precedent.

Furthermore, Professor Choper's words suggest a danger of relying exclusively on the unfettered discretion of the Court for protection of minority interests. History records that the Court has not always been insensitive to political pressure or contemporary fears. To demonstrate this point, I need only mention such cases as *Dred Scott v. Sandford*,[73] *Debs v. United States*,[74] *Whitney v. Cal-*

ifornia,[75] and *Korematsu v. United States.*[76] The names and their lesson are all too familiar. There is, then, the danger that the Court, because of contemporary concerns, could cut back on the individual's protection accorded in earlier decisions. Our best safeguard against the suppression of human liberty—imposed by the Court rather than despite it—is stare decisis. If it is applied with fullest vigor to any transitory desire to contract those rights established by precedent, we can close this gap in the defenses of the "politically impotent minorities." [77]

A third argument that the doctrine of stare decisis grows in its demands when contractions of personal liberty threaten, and lessens its demands to facilitate expansion, rests on a reconsideration of one of the aforementioned basic concerns of stare decisis, namely, reliance interests. In this area of fundamental liberties, and especially in criminal justice, we must not forget whose reliance interests are involved. I have referred to this subject earlier. By way of reminder, I repeat, if the Court overrules to contract liberties, it may convict a man *ex post facto;* [78] he acted in the belief that he was within the law, only to find that the law has changed. If the Court overrules to expand liberties, the prosecutor has lost a case.[79] The balance of reliance interests is clearly not an even one. This notion is not novel; it is the basis of the common law doctrine of strict construction of penal statutes against the government.[80] Thus, reliance considerations pose a weak impediment to an overruling which expands personal liberties, and a strong one to contraction.

Of course, it may be urged that the last argument applies only to "substantive" liberties; a wrongdoer does not act in reliance on an exclusionary rule, for example. I could reply that none of my arguments apply to every sort of case, but together they support an approach to stare decisis of universal application. But here I would also argue that, even in this situation, a consideration of reliance interests compels the same result.

If the Court overrules in order to exclude the fruits of an unconstitutional action, the prosecutor may suffer surprise, but certainly not *unfair* surprise. A good example is *Mapp v. Ohio*,[81] which applied the exclusionary rule of the Fourth Amendment to the states.[82] More than adequate warning had been given a decade previous in *Wolf v. Colorado*,[83] the case which had imposed the "substantive" Fourth Amendment requirements on the states. The primary duty was unchanged by *Mapp;* only the "remedy" was improved. Accordingly, the prosecution could hardly sustain a claim of unfair surprise. If, on the other hand, the Court overrules to admit such fruits, then public expectations—that an effective remedy should exist for a well-understood primary obligation—are disappointed. Again, the balance of reliance interests swings, albeit less decidedly, against overruling to contract preexisting protections.

For my fourth argument I turn to the symbolic importance of the Court's pronouncements. Our system has now been operating under a Supreme Court for almost two centuries. Yet during all that time the Court has never overruled precedent to any significant degree in order to facilitate a significant contraction of human liberties. In arriving at this conclusion, I have excluded consideration of decisions after the Warren era. Since some have been announced recently and others will come, it seems to me it will be more fruitful to test the validity of my statement after the new Court assembles a representative body of precedents.

To be sure, the Court has not been a perfect champion of civil liberties, nor have these rights undergone a continual and steady expansion. There have been periods of stasis, in which the Court refused to recognize rights embodied in the Constitution. *Dred Scott* and *Plessy v. Ferguson*[84] are obvious examples. And there have been periods where the Court has not given prior libertarian cases their fullest and even logical application.

But once fundamental rights have been recognized, there has never been a general reversal of direction by the Court, a going back against the trend of history. Quite understandably, this protracted, monotonic pattern has generated a substantial public expectation of continued growth of constitutional liberties. This expectation is reflected in a quotation from Solicitor General Griswold:

> We take pride in the administration of justice in this country, and rightly so. But it has not always been on the level that it has reached now, and we should hardly be surprised if the present level is not the final one. In each instance, as the level has been raised, those who were then administering justice have been troubled. It is not easy to accept new things, especially when the impetus comes from elsewhere. . . . Throughout history the judges who have been known as great judges have been innovators. . . . Often, there was much grumbling at the time; but in the perspective of history it becomes clear that they have helped to bring our law up to new levels. These are levels of which we soon become proud once we become accustomed to them, and the newness of the new standard wears off.[85]

Existence of this expectation of continued expansion is relevant to the Court's judgment in two ways. The first is that the Court can discount the fears voiced by commentators that expansion of personal liberties will be met by enduring public resistance. As much as the defenders of the status quo may grumble or resent the change, they grow accustomed to the continued growth and, when the "newness" wears off, they come to accept the new status quo. Irrefutable examples here are the reapportionment decisions, long postponed and initially met with a flurry of attacks and criticism, but which went on to be "implemented quickly and with surprisingly little dislocation." [86] It was this turnabout which, as I mentioned above, earned reapportionment the sobriquet of the "success story of the Warren Court." [87] And at least the principle of *Brown v. Board of Education* [88] has been widely enough accepted to permit Georgia's Governor Carter to announce at his recent inauguration: "I say to you quite frankly that the time for racial discrimination is over." [89]

So this expectation of growth of civil liberties weakens in yet another way the stare decisis arguments against overruling to permit expansion. On the other hand, expectation of continued growth counsels in the strongest possible terms against the contraction of liberties. In a sense, contraction would be the total abrogation of stare decisis, because there is *no* substantial precedent for it—the traditional precedent is growth.

I think this lack of precedent for contraction explains the alarm in some quarters when it is suggested that some of the civil liberties decisions are to be reconsidered; and it explains the belief of, say, Professor Charles Reich that we are at "the brink of an authoritarian or police state." [90] This is an obvious overstatement; for confirmation of the fact that we are at present far from such dangers, we need only compare our system with some of the real totalitarian states that exist abroad.[91] Nevertheless, the overreaction is itself instructive. The cries of repression are the result, at least in part, of a long-sustained expectation. Any disappointment of the expectation, any step backward, is subject to a multiplier effect—its symbolic value and the import of the message it communicates will heavily outweigh the corresponding reactions to an equal step forward.[92]

And cries of repression will not be the only result. As a sort of self-fulfilling prophecy, the overreaction of the concerned may induce in others the belief that the Court is sanctioning repression—inviting it and condoning it. The Court plays a most important role in expressing the essential morality inherent in the Constitution. It is the voice not only of what the Constitution commands but also of what it inspires. This responsibility counsels against contracting fundamental rights, since the signal to the nation—the moral message of a reversal of the trend—will be damaging. There is an enormous difference between not opening new frontiers of human liberty and closing ones formerly open, between declining to move forward and legitimating repression.[93]

Furthermore, there is no remedy for the multiplier effect; no carefully worded opinion can lessen the momentousness of an unprecedented reversal of the trend of expanding constitutional rights. Nor can its effects be limited to a single civil right or a single area of civil liberties. Any overruling acts as an admission that some right the Court had formerly called "fundamental" was not so fundamental after all; that admission will undermine the public belief that the other rights labeled fundamental in the past still retain their status. For any contraction by overruling, the Court must pay a huge premium in lost force of those decisions that it wishes to retain as "good constitutional law."

For my fifth and final argument that stare decisis applies with unequal force to contraction and expansion, I leave the theoretical and symbolic for the practicalities of power. In the history of constitutional adjudication, it is well known that the Court first concentrated its efforts on disciplining the federal government's encroachments on the realm of personal liberty, which was constitutionally guaranteed. Only rather recently, in the civil liberties area,[94] has the Court come to emphasize the reach of the Fourteenth Amendment in regulating state action. The reluctance to move earlier in this direction was due in part to a fear of colliding with the power of the states, and this reluctance produced a goodly number of old cases which adopted a restrictive view of individuals' rights vis-à-vis the state. However, we are gradually coming to value individuals' fundamental rights over what in time have proved to be exaggerated sensibilities of the states.[95] Similarly, some older cases relied on a supposed desirability of federalist experimentation. To this position I responded in *Pointer v. Texas*:

> While I quite agree with Mr. Justice Brandeis that "[i]t is one of the happy incidents of the federal system that a . . . State may . . . serve as a laboratory; and try novel social and economic experiments" . . . I do not believe that this includes the power to experiment with the fundamental liberties of citizens safeguarded by the Bill of Rights.[96]

Accordingly, the Warren Court was led to overrule some cases based on such outmoded *ratio decidendi*. While practical considerations counsel against a too rude or too rapid assertion of the power of supervision over the states, common sense reinforces the command of stare decisis not to give back to the states any of their previously asserted power to curtail fundamental liberties— power which was denied to them by the Fourteenth Amendment. Nothing is to be gained by overruling those cases which caused wounds to state sensibilities that have already healed.

Similar practicalities are involved when consideration shifts from the states to public opinion. As the quotation of Solicitor General Griswold showed, the majority often resents the expansion of individual rights. This usually represents more an imagined than a real danger to the Court. But even assuming *arguendo* that a Court conscious of its role in society should take public opinion into account, what effect should this practicality have on a proposed contraction of rights? Once the advance in constitutional rights has been made and the "newness of the new standard wears off," the tough part with respect to public opinion is past; and again stare decisis and common sense preclude retreat. That is, the reasons that counseled inertia evaporate once a move forward has been made, leaving no reason to later move backward. Thus, the arguments for respecting precedent are further strengthened when contraction of rights is in issue.

The impact of stare decisis on our constitutional safeguards, then, results in a ratchet-like effect. Under its dictates, the Court can readily move to expand those liberties, as the Constitution properly conceived mandates, but contraction meets stiffer resistance. And, as suggested, this concept of stare decisis both justifies the overruling involved in the expansion of human liberties during the Warren years and counsels against the future overruling of the Warren Court libertarian decisions.

To close on a harmonious note, I would like to note the interesting parallel that exists in terms of the power of the legislature and executive in constitutional interpretation. They, under the constraints of the Constitution rather than stare decisis, can expand but not contract the people's fundamental liberties.[97] Or, as explained in *Katzenbach v. Morgan*,[98] they may enforce or expand existing rights, but they have "no power to restrict, abrogate, or dilute these guarantees."

It is thus the wisdom of our system to close the loophole—to impose an impediment to the possibility of repression by the judiciary—by means of stare decisis. Instead of the inflexibility of a constitutional prohibition on judicial abrogation of personal rights, we interpose only the commands of this doctrine. For it would be unthinkable that we absolutely forbid all three branches from correcting a faulty constitutional interpretation—that would only serve to induce a paralytic caution on the part of the judiciary. The fear of going off in the wrong direction would induce the Court to foreswear going forward at all. The virtue of stare decisis is that "the compulsion of exigency of the doctrine is in the last analysis, moral and intellectual rather than arbitrary or inflexible." [99] But, as I have tried to show, the moral compulsion it exerts is a strong one—more than strong enough to shelter the fundamental civil liberties decisions of the Warren Court.)

NOTES

I. A COURT OF RELEVANT JUSTICE

1. My references to the Warren Court are intended to denote the era of Supreme Court history stretching from Brown v. Board of Education, 347 U.S. 483 (1954) to the retirement of Earl Warren in June, 1969.
2. Dred Scott v. Sandford, 60 U.S. (19 How.) 393 (1857).
3. 369 U.S. 186 (1962).
4. 377 U.S. 533 (1964).
5. E.g., Burton v. Wilmington Parking Authority, 365 U.S. 715 (1961); Cooper v. Aaron, 358 U.S. 1 (1958); Brown v. Board of Educ., 347 U.S. 483 (1954).
6. McKay, *Reapportionment: Success Story of the Warren Court*, 67 Mich. L. Rev. 223 (1968).
7. 351 U.S. 12 (1956).
8. *Id.* at 19 (Black, J., plurality opinion).

9. See Report of the Attorney General's Committee on Poverty and the Administration of Federal Criminal Justice 104–7 and n. 69 (1963).

10. Pye, *The Warren Court and Criminal Procedure*, 67 Mich. L. Rev. 249, 258 (1968).

11. See Johnson v. Zerbst, 304 U.S. 458 (1938).

12. Betts v. Brady, 316 U.S. 455 (1942).

13. Gideon v. Wainwright, 372 U.S. 335 (1963); see Junker, *The Right to Counsel in Misdemeanor Cases*, 43 Wash. L. Rev. 685, 687 (1968).

14. Lewis, Gideon's Trumpet 237 (1964).

15. 378 U.S. 478 (1964).

16. 367 U.S. 643 (1961).

17. 378 U.S. at 492.

18. *Id.* at 487.

19. *Ex parte* Sullivan, 107 F. Supp. 514, 517–18 (D. Utah 1952) (footnote omitted), quoted in 378 U.S. at 488.

20. 372 U.S. at 335.

21. 384 U.S. 436 (1966).

22. *Id.* at 471.

23. 338 U.S. 25, 27–28 (1949).

24. 367 U.S. at 655–56.

25. *Id.* at 660.

26. 389 U.S. 347 (1967).

27. See Silverman v. United States, 365 U.S. 505 (1961); Goldman v. United States, 316 U.S. 129 (1942); Olmstead v. United States, 277 U.S. 438 (1928).

28. See Rios v. United States, 364 U.S. 253 (1960) (taxicab); Jones v. United States, 362 U.S. 257 (1960) (friend's apartment); Hester v. United States, 265 U.S. 57 (1924) (open field is not protected); Silverthorne Lumber Co. v. United States, 251 U.S. 385 (1920) (business office).

29. Weems v. United States, 217 U.S. 349, 373 (1910).

30. Olmstead v. United States, 277 U.S. 438, 474 (1928) (dissenting opinion).
31. 389 U.S. at 351–52.
32. *Id.* at 353.
33. 339 U.S. 56, 66 (1950).
34. 395 U.S. 752 (1969).
35. *Id.* at 763.
36. 387 U.S. 294 (1967).
37. Gouled v. United States, 255 U.S. 298 (1921); Boyd v. United States, 116 U.S. 616 (1886).
38. 387 U.S. at 304.
39. Gouled v. United States, 255 U.S. 298 (1921); see Cushman, Cases in Civil Liberties 169 (1968).
40. 211 U.S. 78 (1908).
41. Pointer v. Texas, 380 U.S. 400, 413 (1965) (Goldberg, J., concurring).
42. *Id.* at 411–12 (Goldberg, J., concurring).
43. Pointer v. Texas, 380 U.S. 400 (1965).
44. Pye, *supra* note 10 at 258.
45. See Escobedo v. Illinois, 378 U.S. 478, 490 (1964) (Goldberg, J.).
46. See, e.g., Bickel, The Supreme Court and the Idea of Progress 117–51 (1970); Black, *The Lawfulness of the Segregation Decisions*, 69 Yale L. J. 421 (1960); Carter, *The Warren Court and Desegregation*, 67 Mich. L. Rev. 237 (1968); Kauper, *Segregation in Public Education*, 52 Mich. L. Rev. 1137 (1954); Wechsler, *Toward Neutral Principles of Constitutional Law*, 73 Harv. L. Rev. 1, 26–34 (1959).
47. See generally Bickel, *The Decade of School Desegregation: Progress and Prospects*, 64 Colum. L. Rev. 193 (1964).
48. See, e.g., Griffin v. County School Bd., 377 U.S. 218

(1964) (closing of public schools and state support of private, segregated schools); Goss v. Board of Educ., 373 U.S. 683 (1963) (student transfer plan); Felder v. Harnett County Board of Educ., 349 F. 2d 366 (4th Cir. 1965) (freedom of choice).

49. Hamilton v. Alabama, 376 U.S. 650 (1964), *rev'g mem.* *Ex parte* Hamilton, 275 Ala. 574, 156 So. 2d 926 (1963).

50. 377 U.S. at 533, 562.

51. *In re* Gault, 387 U.S. 1 (1967).

52. 380 U.S. 479 (1965). But see Younger v. Harris, 39 U.S.L.W. 4201 (U.S. Feb. 23, 1971).

53. E.g., Shapiro v. Thompson, 394 U.S. 618 (1969); King v. Smith, 392 U.S. 309 (1968).

54. Illinois v. Allen, 397 U.S. 337, 346–47 (1970) (Black, J.), noted in *The Supreme Court, 1969 Term*, 84 Harv. L. Rev. 1, 90–100 (1970).

55. But see Pennsylvania v. Tate, 39 U.S.L.W. 2499 (Pa. Sup. Ct. Feb. 16, 1971).

56. Hawkins v. Town of Shaw, 39 U.S.L.W. 2431 (5th Cir. Jan. 28, 1971).

57. See McInnis v. Ogilvie, 394 U.S. 322 (1969), *aff'g mem.* McInnis v. Shapiro, 293 F. Supp. 327 (N.D. Ill. 1968).

58. Wyman v. James, 39 U.S.L.W. 4085 (U.S. Jan. 12, 1971) (home visits by welfare caseworker).

II. JUDICIAL ACTIVISM AND STRICT CONSTRUCTIONISM

1. 376 U.S. 681, 728 (1964).

2. Bell v. Maryland, 378 U.S. 226 (1964).

3. See e.g. United States v. Barnett, 376 U.S. 681, 728

(Goldberg, J., dissenting). Black & Cahn, *Justice Black and First Amendment "Absolutes": A Public Interview*, 37 N.Y.U.L. Rev. 549 (1962) & *cf.* Griswold v. Connecticut, 381 U.S. 479, 507 (1965) (Black, J., dissenting).

4. Home Building Association v. Blaisdell, 290 U.S. 398, 448-49 (1934) (Sutherland, J., dissenting).
5. Blodgett v. Holden, 275 U.S. 142, 148 (1927) (separate opinion of Holmes, J.).
6. 372 U.S. 144, 159 (1963).
7. 198 U.S. 45 (1905).
8. *Id.* at 75, 76.
9. 83 U.S. (16 Wall.) 36, 71 (1873).
10. 113 U.S. 27, 31 (1885).
11. Goldberg, The Defenses of Freedom 44, 45 (Moynihan ed. 1966). See also the excellent exposition of this theme in depth in Robert Harris, The Quest for Equality 109–30 (1960).
12. See generally Freund, The Supreme Court of the United States 86–87 (1961).
13. Shapiro v. Thompson, 394 U.S. 618 (1969).
14. E.g., Gomillion v. Lightfoot, 364 U.S. 339 (1960).
15. Carrington v. Rash, 380 U.S. 89 (1965).
16. Harper v. Virginia Board of Elections, 383 U.S. 663 (1966).
17. Niebuhr, The Children of Light and the Children of Darkness 74 (1953), quoted in Freund, *supra* note 12, at 83.
18. See *Developments in the Law—Equal Protection*, 82 Harv. L. Rev. 1065, 1087 (1969).
19. II Kennedy, Memoirs of William Wirt 256 (1856).
20. 31 U.S. (6 Pet.) 515 (1832).
21. I Warren, The Supreme Court in United States History 756 (1935).

22. Dred Scott v. Sandford, 60 U.S. (19 How.) 393 (1857).
23. Hosokawa, Nisei 276 (1969).
24. Korematsu v. United States, 323 U.S. 214 (1944).
25. *Id.* at 246.
26. *Id.* at 233.
27. 163 U.S. 537 (1896).
28. E.g., Cumming v. Richmond County Board of Educ., 175 U.S. 528 (1899).
29. 163 U.S. at 559–60.
30. 10 U.S. (6 Cranch) 87 (1810).
31. Annals 12th Cong. 2d Sess. 856–59, quoted in Beveridge, Life of John Marshall 599 (1919).
32. E.g., Engel v. Vitale, 370 U.S. 421 (1962).
33. Quoted in Goldberg, The Defenses of Freedom 150 (1966).
34. Hawkins v. Town of Shaw, 39 U.S.L.W. 2431 (5th Cir. Jan. 28, 1971).
35. Time Magazine, Jan. 18, 1971, at 49, col. 3.
36. United States v. Sinclair, 8 BNA Cr. L. Rep. 2321 (E.D. Mich. Jan. 25, 1971); United States v. Smith 8 BNA Cr. L. Rep. 226 (C.D. Calif. Jan. 8, 1971).
37. Hand, *The Contribution of an Independent Judiciary to Civilization,* quoted in Freund, *supra* note 12, at 87–88.

III. A NEW THEORY OF CONSTITUTIONAL STARE DECISIS

1. Bridges v. California, 314 U.S. 252, 289 (1941) (dissenting opinion).
2. See Goldberg, *The Court Sits—In the Center of the Storm,* N.Y. Times Magazine, Nov. 8, 1964, at 30.

3. However, my exasperation never matched that of Professor Jesse Choper, who launched a counterattack on "the massive volume of uninformed, unthinking, unbridled, largely undocumented, and generally unsound carping and baiting that has been placed, mainly by irresponsible and legally ignorant attackers, under the heading of 'criticism.'" *On the Warren Court and Judicial Review*, 17 Cath. U.L. Rev. 20, 20 (1967).

4. See the articles collected in Wright, *Professor Bickel, the Scholarly Tradition, and the Supreme Court*, 84 Harv. L. Rev. 769, 770 nn.4 & 5 (1971).

5. 5 U.S. (1 Cranch) 137 (1803); see Choper, *supra* note 3, at 22–27.

6. Bickel, The Least Dangerous Branch 18 (1962); see *id.* 16–23; Goldberg and Dershowitz, *Declaring the Death Penalty Unconstitutional*, 83 Harv. L. Rev. 1773, 1777 (1970).

7. See Hand, The Bill of Rights 27–29 (1958).

8. See Goldberg, *supra* note 2.

9. Act of Sept. 24, 1789, ch. 20, 1 Stat. 85.

10. Black, The People and the Court 23 (1960).

11. See, e.g., Wechsler, *Toward Neutral Principles of Constitutional Law*, 73 Harv. L. Rev. 1, 3–5 (1959).

12. Bickel, *supra* note 6, at 17.

13. Other constraints suggested by Professor Bickel include the appointment power, the general political climate, the judges' good common sense, and the necessity—to render the judges' views effective—of acquiring the assent of the political institutions and of the people. Bickel, The Supreme Court and the Idea of Progress 88–91 (1970). See also Bickel, *supra* note 6, at 34–72.

14. Bickel, The Supreme Court and the Idea of Progress 81 (1970).

15. See, e.g., Bickel, *supra* note 6, at 23–28, 49–65; Bickel,

supra note 14, at 81–100; Hart, *The Supreme Court, 1958 Term, Foreword: The Time Chart of the Justices*, 73 Harv. L. Rev. 84, 99 (1959); Wechsler, *supra* note 11, at 10–20.

16. Bickel, *supra* note 14, at 86.
17. *Id.* at 58.
18. Kurland, *The Supreme Court, 1963 Term, Foreword: Equal in Origin and Equal in Title to the Legislative and Executive Branches of the Government*, 78 Harv. L. Rev. 143, 144–45 (1964).
19. Wright, *The Supreme Court Today*, 3 Trial, April–May (1967), at 10–11.
20. Cox, The Warren Court 21 (1968).
21. For the historical background of the doctrine in the common law see Catlett, *The Development of the Doctrine of Stare Decisis and the Extent to Which It Should Be Applied*, 21 Wash. L. Rev. 158–60 (1946); Lobingier, *Precedent in Past and Present Legal Systems*, 44 Mich. L. Rev. 955–65 (1946).
22. Lile, *Some Views on the Rule of Stare Decisis*, 4 Va. L. Rev. 95, 97 (1916).
23. See generally Lobingier, *supra* note 21, at 955–966.
24. See generally Hughes, The Supreme Court of the United States 52 (1928).
25. See Bickel, *supra* note 14, at 82.
26. Cf. Goldberg, *Government Under Law*, 40 Chi.-Kent L. Rev. 1, 2 (1963); The Federalist No. 78, at 490 (1888) (Hamilton).
27. Cardozo, The Nature of the Judicial Process 149 (1937); *cf.* Hand, The Spirit of Liberty 241 (2d ed. 1953).
28. But cf Lobingier, *supra* note 21, at 965–66; Pound, *The Status of the Rule of Judicial Precedent, Survey of Con-*

ference Problems, 14 U. Cinn. L. Rev. 324, 328–32 (1940).

29. Chamberlain, *The Doctrine of Stare Decisis as Applied to Decisions of Constitutional Questions,* 3 Harv. L. Rev. 125, 130–31 (1889); Shroder, *The Doctrine of Stare Decisis—Its Application to Decisions Involving Constitutional Interpretation,* 58 Cent. L. J. 23, 28–31 (1904); Brown, *Construing the Constitution: A Trial Lawyer's Plea for* Stare Decisis, 44 A.B.A.J. 742 (1958). But see Catlett, *supra* note 21, at 163–64; Lobingier, *supra* note 21, at 974.

30. Reed, *Stare Decisis and Constitutional Law,* 35 Pa. Bar. Assn. Q., 131, 134 6 (1938). Interestingly enough, the argument has also been made that stare decisis is inapplicable to constitutional law because it implies too *much* flexibility to overrule. Long, *The Doctrine of Stare Decisis: Misapplied to Constitutional Law,* 45 A.B.A.J. 921, 923–24 (1959).

31. Burnet v. Coronado Oil & Gas Co., 285 U.S. 393, 406–8 (1932) (Brandeis, J., dissenting); see Washington v. W. C. Dawson & Co., 264 U.S. 219, 237–39 (1924) (Brandeis, J., dissenting).

32. 285 U.S. at 393, 412 (1932) (Brandeis, J., dissenting).

33. Douglas, *Stare Decisis,* 49 Colum. L. Rev. 735, 754 (1949).

34. Smith v. Allwright, 321 U.S. 649 (1944) (state cannot racially discriminate in primary election), *overruling* Grovey v. Townsend, 295 U.S. 45 (1935); Jones v. Opelika, 319 U.S. 103 (1943) (striking down a license tax on dissemination of religious literature), *vacating* Jones v. Opelika, 316 U.S. 584 (1942); Board of Educ. v. Barnette, 319 U.S. 624 (1943) (state cannot require flag salute in opposition to religious beliefs), *overruling*

Minersville School Dist. v. Gobitis, 310 U.S. 586 (1940); Kilbourn v. Thompson, 103 U.S. 168 (1880) (Congress cannot commit for contempt following refusal to obey order in congressional investigation), *overruling* Anderson v. Dunn, 19 U.S. (6 Wheat.) 204 (1821).

35. While for my purposes here I assume that stare decisis is weaker in the socioeconomic sphere, it should be noted that some would argue that the involvement of property rights in a constitutional question calls for a stricter application of the doctrine; the theory is that reliance interests are likely to be stronger. See, e.g., Noland, *Stare Decisis and the Overruling of Constitutional Decisions in the Warren Years*, 4 Val. U. L. Rev. 101, 107 (1969). Certainly, this theory is accepted in cases not of constitutional stature. See T. S. Faulk & Co. v. Boutwell, 7 So. 2d 490, 491, 242 Ala. 526, 527–28 (1942); Catlett, *supra* note 21, at 163.

36. See Griswold v. Connecticut, 381 U.S. 479, 497 (1965) (Goldberg, J., concurring); Goldberg and Dershowitz, *supra* note 6, at 1785.

37. One factor uniquely present in constitutional adjudication is that the Court's decision is for practical purposes beyond correction by legislative action. See Burnet v. Coronado Oil & Gas Co., 285 U.S. 393, 405–7 (1932) (Brandeis, J., dissenting). While this factor does not detract from the five reasons supporting stare decisis, it does counsel a more flexible approach to the doctrine in constitutional cases. This flexibility is stressed in the immediately following text. See Brown, *supra* note 29, at 743.

38. Pollock v. Farmer's Loan & Trust Co., 157 U.S. 429, 652 (1895) (White, J., dissenting), *vacated on rehearing*, 158 U.S. 601 (1895).

39. See Chamberlain, The Doctrine of State Decisis 19

(1885) quoted in Catlett, *supra* note 21, at 161; Llewellyn, The Bramble Bush 156–60 (2d ed. 1951); Lobingier, *supra* note 21, at 976–80. See also Catlett, *supra* note 21; Wright, *Precedents*, 4 Toronto L. J. 247 (1942).

40. See Helvering v. Hallock, 309 U.S. 106, 119 (1940) (Frankfurter, J.).

41. United States v. South-Eastern Underwriters Assn., 322 U.S. 533, 580 (1944) (Stone, C. J., dissenting); see *id.* at 594 (Jackson, J., dissenting).

42. Holmes, The Common Law 36 (1881).

43. The statistics of one writer suggest that the Warren Court was significantly more inclined to overrule than prior Courts. Noland, *supra* note 35, at 119. However, his definitional criteria differ from those of the earlier studies on which his comparison rests; moreover, his own statistics are plagued by internal inconsistencies. Compare *id.* at 119, with *id.* at 132–35. While precise conclusions are thus precluded, his general conclusion may still be correct. However, Professor Choper suggests that the Warren Court was no more activist, with regard to overruling precedents, than the Vinson and Stone Courts. See Choper, *supra* note 3, at 22–24.

44. See London Street Tramways, Ltd. v. London County Council, [1898] A.C. 375, 380–81 (dictum); 1 Kent's Commentaries 475 (14th ed. 1896); Lobingier, *supra* note 21, at 973; Shroder, *supra* note 29, at 28 (suggests testing precedent like jury verdict: could anyone reasonably arrive at same conclusion?).

45. 378 U.S. 52 (1964).

46. 284 U.S. 141 (1931) (federal government could compel testimony incriminating under state law).

47. United States v. Saline Bank, 26 U.S. (1 Pet.) 100 (1828).

48. Ballman v. Fagin, 200 U.S. 186 (1906).

49. 61 Eng. Rep. 116 (Ch. 1851).

50. United States v. McRae, L. R. 3 Ch. App. 79 (1867).

51. See 378 U.S. at 76–77.

52. 357 U.S. 371 (1958).

53. 378 U.S. 1 (1964).

54. Compare the ancient "mischief rule" of statutory construction. See Heydon's Case, 76 Eng. Rep. 637 (Ex. 1584).

55. Fortson v. Morris, 385 U.S. 231, 248 n. 5 (1966) (Fortas, J., dissenting) (equal protection); Miranda v. Arizona, 384 U.S. 436, 443–44 (1966) (Warren, C. J.); Estes v. Texas, 381 U.S. 532, 564 (1965) (Warren, C. J., concurring) (Sixth and Fourteenth Amendments); Bell v. Maryland, 378 U.S. 226, 298 n. 17 (1964) (Goldberg, J., concurring) (Fourteenth Amendment); Poe v. Ullman, 367 U.S. 497, 551 (1961) (Harlan, J., dissenting) (Fourth Amendment).

56. 217 U.S. 349, 373 (1910) (emphasis added).

57. See generally Goldberg, *Equality and Governmental Action*, 39 N.Y.U.L. Rev. 205 (1964).

58. 83 U.S. (16 Wall.) 36, 81 (1873). See The Civil Rights Cases, 109 U.S. 3 (1883).

59. Justice Miller's resistance to judicial expansion of personal liberties is further shown in *ex parte* Garland, 71 U.S. (4 Wall.) 333, 390, 392, 399 (1867) (dissenting opinion) (*ex post facto* laws).

60. The most immediate development was the use of the equal protection clause to protect economic interests, including those of corporations. See Santa Clara County v. Southern Pac. Ry., 118 U.S. 394, 396 (1886); cf. Morey v. Doud, 354 U.S. 457 (1957).

61. See, e.g., Reynolds v. Sims, 377 U.S. 533 (1964).

62. See e.g., Gideon v. Wainwright, 372 U.S. 335 (1963);

Griffin v. Illinois, 351 U.S. 12 (1956); cf. Goldberg, *Preface: Symposium, Governmental Compensation for Victims of Violence,* 43 So. Calif. L. Rev. 1, 2–3 (1970).

63. See *In re* Kemmler, 136 U.S. 436, 446–47 (1890); Granucci, *"Nor Cruel and Unusual Punishments Inflicted": The Original Meaning,* 57 Calif. L. Rev. 839 (1969).

64. Trop v. Dulles, 356 U.S. 86, 101 (1958).

65. *Id.*

66. Robinson v. California, 370 U.S. 660 (1962).

67. 313 U.S. 299, 316 (1941).

68. Ralph v. Warden, 39 U.S.L.W. 2331 (4th Cir., Dec. 22, 1970); cf. Rudolph v. Alabama, 375 U.S. 889 (1963) (Goldberg, J., dissenting to denial of certiorari).

69. See Goldberg & Dershowitz, *supra* note 6.

70. McCulloch v. Maryland, 17 U.S. (4 Wheat.) 316, 407 (1819).

71. Olmstead v. United States, 277 U.S. 438, 472 (1928) (dissenting opinion).

72. Choper, *supra* note 3, at 40 (footnotes omitted).

73. 60 U.S. (19 How.) 393 (1857).

74. 249 U.S. 211 (1919).

75. 274 U.S. 357 (1927).

76. 323 U.S. 214 (1944).

77. Rostow, *The Democratic Character of Judicial Review,* 66 Harv. L. Rev. 193, 202 (1952), quoted in Choper, *supra* note 3, at 40.

78. See Catlett, *supra* note 21, at 163.

79. A weightier reliance interest of the state may be present. The overruling could affect the validity of many previous cases, which could then be challenged by habeas corpus. However, this reliance interest can be accommodated by limiting retroactivity in appropriate cases.

80. See McBoyle v. United States, 283 U.S. 25 (1931) (Holmes, J.).

81. 367 U.S. 643 (1961).

82. *Id.* at 655.

83. 338 U.S. 25 (1949).

84. 163 U.S. 537 (1896), *overruled*, Brown v. Board of Educ., 347 U.S. 483 (1954); see Browder v. Gayle, 142 F. Supp. 707, 717 (M.D. Ala. 1956), *aff'd per curiam*, 352 U.S. 903 (1956).

85. Griswold, *The Long View*, 51 A.B.A.J. 1017, 1018 (1965).

86. McKay, *Reapportionment: Success Story of the Warren Court*, 67 Mich. L. Rev. 223, 225 (1968).

87. See *id.*

88. 347 U.S. 483 (1954).

89. Time Magazine, Feb. 1, 1971, at 20, col. 3.

90. Reich, The Greening of America 300 (1970), reviewed, Dershowitz, Civil Liberties, Feb. 1971, at 2.

91. See London, The Confession (1971), reviewed, Dershowitz, N.Y. Times Book Review, Feb. 7, 1971, at 5.

92. Without analyzing the merits of the decision, the widespread press and public reaction to the Court's February 24, 1971, decision in Harris v. New York tends to confirm the validity of this statement. 39 U.S.L.W. 4281 (U.S. Feb. 24, 1971).

93. See e.g., Korematsu v. United States, 323 U.S. 214, 245–46 (1944) (Jackson, J., dissenting); Bickel, *supra* note 6, at 128–33.

94. On the other hand, the Court has withdrawn from supervision of state power in economic matters. See Ferguson v. Skrupa, 372 U.S. 726 (1963).

95. E.g., compare Mapp v. Ohio, 367 U.S. 643 (1961), with Wolf v. Colorado, 338 U.S. 25 (1949).

96. 380 U.S. 400, 413 (1965) (concurring opinion) (citation omitted).

97. Goldberg and Dershowitz, *supra* note 6, at 1807–13. See Cooper v. Aaron, 358 U.S. 1 (1958).

98. 384 U.S. 641, 651–52 n. 10 (1966); see Shapiro v. Thompson, 394 U.S. 618, 641 (1969). While *Morgan* explicitly referred only to congressional power under section five of the Fourteenth Amendment, its principle logically extends to the treatment of all civil liberties at the hands of legislatures and executives on both the federal and state level.

     The fundamental nature of this principle is shown by the fact that in the *body* of the Constitution—which was not otherwise focused on personal liberties—the framers made this rachet effect explicit with respect to the Great Writ of habeas corpus; this was expressed in the suspension clause. U.S. Const. art. I, §9, cl. 2. Its workings are explored in the excellent discussion contained in *Developments in the Law—Federal Habeas Corpus*, 83 Harv. L. Rev. 1038, 1266–74 (1970).

99. Quoted in Catlett, *supra* note 21, at 161. Furthermore, the necessity for overruling can be minimized if the Court makes its advances in a cautious and tentative manner. Thus, in Miranda v. Arizona, 384 U.S. 436, 390 (1966), the Court asserted only a principle, while inviting Congress and the states to experiment in the details of effectuation.

PUBLISHED ROSENTHAL
LECTURES 1948–1971

1948   Hazard, John N. "The Soviet Union and International Law," *Illinois Law Review*, XLIII, 591.

1949   Freund, Paul A. *On Understanding the Supreme Court*. Boston: Little, Brown & Co.

1951   Dawson, John P. *Unjust Enrichment, A Comparative Analysis*. Boston: Little, Brown & Co.

1952   Feller, Abraham H. *United Nations and World Community*. Boston: Little, Brown & Co.

1952   Horsky, Charles A. *The Washington Lawyer*. Boston: Little, Brown & Co.

1953   Vanderbilt, Arthur T. "The Essentials of A Sound Judical System," *Northwestern University Law Review*, XLVIII.

1954   Berle, Adolf A., Jr. *The Twentieth Century Capitalist Revolution*. New York: Harcourt, Brace.

1956   Hurst, James W. *Law and the Conditions of Freedom in the Nineteenth Century United States*. Madison: University of Wisconsin Press.

1956   Sohn, Louis B. "United Nations Charter Revision and the Rule of Law: A Program for Peace," *Northwestern University Law Review*, L, 709.

1956   Gross, Ernest A. "Major Problems in Disarmament," *Northwestern University Law Review*, LI, 299.

1956   Parker, John J. "Dual Sovereignty and the Federal Courts," *Northwestern University Law Review*, LI, 407.

1957   Ukai, Nobushige. "The Individual and the Rule of Law Under the New Japanese Constitution," *Northwestern University Law Review*, LI, 733.

1957   Papale, Antonia Edward. "Judicial Enforcement of Desegregation: Its Problems and Limitations," *Northwestern University Law Review*, LII, 301.

1957   Hart, Herbert L. A. "Murder and the Principles of Punishment: England and the United States," *Northwestern University Law Review*, LII, 433.

1958   Green, Leon. *Traffic Victims: Tort Law and Insurance*. Evanston, Ill.: Northwestern University Press.

1960   Radcliffe, Cyril John. *The Law and Its Compass*. Evanston, Ill.: Northwestern University Press.

1961   Eisenstein, Louis. *The Ideologies of Taxation*. New York: Ronald Press.

1961   Havighurst, Harold C. *The Nature of Private Contract*. Evanston, Ill.: Northwestern University Press.

1962   Pike, James Albert. *Beyond the Law: The Religious and Ethical Meaning of the Lawyer's Vocation*. New York: Doubleday and Co.

1964 Katz, Wilber G. *Religion and American Constitutions.* Evanston, Ill.: Northwestern University Press.

1965 Cowen, Zelman. *The British Commonwealth of Nations in a Changing World: Law, Politics, and Prospects.* Evanston, Ill.: Northwestern University Press.

1967 Schaefer, Walter V. *The Suspect and Society: Criminal Procedure and Converging Constitutional Doctrines.* Evanston, Ill.: Northwestern University Press.

1967 Freedman, Max, Beaney, William M., and Rostow, Eugene V. *Perspectives on the Court.* Evanston, Ill.: Northwestern University Press.

1968 Donner, André M. *The Role of the Lawyer in the European Communities.* Evanston, Ill.: Northwestern University Press.

1969 McGowan, Carl. *The Organization of Judicial Power in the United States.* Evanston, Ill.: Northwestern University Press.

1969 Jones, Harry W. *The Efficacy of Law.* Evanston, Ill.: Northwestern University Press.

1971 Goldberg, Arthur J. *Equal Justice: The Warren Era of the Supreme Court.* Evanston, Ill.: Northwestern University Press.